Reviews of other title

"Read one of New Zealand author Mary Jane Walker's informed and richly entertaining travel books and the thirst for more adventures leads to searching for additional volumes."

Grady Harp, Amazon Hall of Fame reviewer, from a review of *A Maverick Traveller Anthology,* 20 April 2019

'Do take a walk with Mary Jane Walker!'

"In the tradition of Gertrude Bell, Freya Stark, Isabella Bird and other adventurous women, Mary Jane Walker's relationship with the world is one of insatiable curiosity. She is driven to immerse herself in experience. I was happy to walk with Walker around the world, and was pulled in by her prose."

Brooklyn Stooptalk, from an Amazon review of *A Maverick Traveller,* 20 April 2018

'Marvellous Information!!!!'

"Just an enriching book on a place I knew very little about. I've always said that the purpose of reading is acquiring new knowledge & I did."

D. West, from an Amazon review of *A Maverick New Zealand Way*, 22 May 2019

'Awesome book and genuine writing style'

"Awesome book and genuine writing style. As a recent traveler to Cuba myself, I really appreciate how the author really embeds herself in the Cuban culture and stories that make the country so special. Great read (with great pictures). Would definitely recommend!"

Giancarlo Cozzi, review of *A Maverick Cuban Way*, Amazon Kindle edition, 15 November 2017

"Thank you, Mary Jane. You have done all of us—wanderers and "sedentarians" alike—a tremendous service.

From an Amazon review of *A Maverick Pilgrim Way* by R. Russell Bittner, 29 April 2018.

"A Maverick USA Way is a unique approach to travelling the US. Author Mary Jane Walker describes being fairly sure even before she arrived that Donald Trump would [win] and she weaves political explorations into her travels, making this much more in depth than the average travel diary... A particularly pertinent chapter covers her visit to Standing Rock... "

Renee Jones, review of *A Maverick USA Way* on Goodreads, 16 December 2017. Minor typographical corrections.

'An Interesting Travel Memoir'

"A Maverick Himalayan Way by adventurer and author Mary Jane Walker is a very interesting travel memoir. "

From a review of *A Maverick Himalayan Way,* new edition, by 'Piaras', Amazon Vine Voice reviewer, 24 May 2019

'Viking's Way'

"Mary Jane Walker does it again, I just love all her books."

'Deha', From an Amazon review of *A Maverick Inuit Way and the Vikings,* 28 March 2019

MARY JANE WALKER

MARY JANE WALKER

Mary Jane Walker is a New Zealand-based maverick and author, born with a wanderlust gene.

Mary Jane has spent two years naked on a Chinese Junk; got so lost she ended up in Robin Hood's hiding-place; drunk hallucinogenic tea in the Amazon rainforest; and kicked a nuclear-powered submarine.

She has travelled much of the world and has incredible stories to share about her adventures. There is more to travelling than boutique restaurants and fancy hotels.

She has walked to Mount Everest Base Camp and seen the work and life of Sherpas. Danced and prayed in many churches, temples and mosques. Traversed various parts of the Camino de Europa. Explored the stunning landscapes of New Zealand. Visited remote parts of the Arctic while pulled by a team of dogs. And all while meeting amazing people along the way.

The urge to explore is not just something that's in us: for some people it's really in us. So, for a richer travelling experience, not just about countries but their people and histories as well, read on.

Email: maryjanewalker@a-maverick.com
Facebook:
facebook.com/amavericktraveller
Instagram: @a_maverick_traveller
Linkedin: Mary Jane Walker
Pinterest: amavericktraveller
Twitter: @Mavericktravel0

www.a-maverick.com

MARY JANE WALKER

Other books by Mary Jane Walker

A Maverick Traveller

A Maverick Traveller is a funny, interesting adventure compilation of Mary Jane's adventures. Starting from her beginnings in travel it follows her through a life filled with exploration of cultures, mountains, histories and more. Whether it was eating dog unintentionally in Indonesia, meeting the rapper 50 Cent at a backpackers' hostel or kicking a US nuclear submarine in New Zealand, A Maverick Traveller is filled with the unique stories and experiences of Mary Jane Walker.

A Maverick New Zealand Way

Finalist in Travel at the International Book Awards, 2018. Discover the stunning back country of New Zealand. Come along with Mary Jane on over fifty walks and mountain ascents throughout the islands of New Zealand. Offering an interesting account of New Zealand history and urban development alongside tales of modern-day adventure, it is the perfect read to inspire you to get outdoors in New Zealand.

A Maverick Cuban Way

Trek with Mary Jane to Fidel's revolutionary hideout in the Sierra Maestra. See where the world nearly ended and the Bay of Pigs and have coffee looking at the American Guantánamo Base, all the while doing a salsa to the Buena Vista Social Club. Go to where Columbus first landed but don't expect to have wifi on your phone, only in hotspots using a card. People are proud and there's one doctor for every 150 people. Mary Jane loved it and did it.

A Maverick Pilgrim Way

Pilgrim trails are not just for the religious! Follow the winding ancient roads of pilgrims across the continent of Europe and the Mediterranean, and explore their hinterlands as well. Mary Jane will keep returning to complete more and more of these culturally significant routes.

A Maverick USA Way

Mary Jane took Amtrak trains around America and visited Glacier, Yellowstone, Grand Teton, Rocky Mountain and Yosemite National Parks before the snow hit. She loved the Smithsonian museums and after seeing a live dance at the American Indian Museum, she decided to go to Standing Rock. It was a protest over land rights and drinking water, at 30 below zero! She loved Detroit which is going back to being a park, and Galveston and Birmingham, Alabama. She was there during the election and was not surprised Trump won. She was tired of being mistaken for being a homeless person because she had a backpack and left San Francisco because of it.

A Maverick Himalayan Way

Mary Jane walked for ninety days and nights throughout the Himalayan region and Nepal, a part of the world loaded with adventures and discoveries of culture, the people, their religions and the beautiful landscapes. She visited the Hindu Kush in Pakistan and listened to the Dalai Lama in Sikkim, India. It is a journey of old and new. So, come trekking in the Himalayas with Mary Jane.

A Maverick Inuit Way and the Vikings

Mary Jane's adventures in the Arctic take her dog sledding in Greenland, exploring glaciers and icebergs in Iceland, and meeting some interesting locals. She found herself stuck on a ship in the freezing Arctic Ocean amongst icebergs, and had her car windows almost blown out by gale force winds! Take a ride through the Arctic and its fascinating history.

The Scottish Isles: Shetlands, Orkneys and Hebrides (Part 1)

Mary Jane visits the Shetland and Orkney groups of islands, to the north of the Scottish mainland. These exotic islands have quite a different culture and history to most of the mainland, with evidence of an ancient civilisation on the Orkneys and a history of Norse colonisation on both sets of islands. She also visits several islands of the Inner Hebrides.

Catchy Cyprus (forthcoming)

This is a short book based on my visit to Cyprus, the island that copper's named after. A former British possession in the Mediterranean Sea, Cyprus is divided into Greek-dominated and Turkish-dominated regions with United Nations troops in between. A surprisingly large amount of the island remains under the Union Jack as well.

Lonely Lebanon (forthcoming)

I also visited the small country of Lebanon, north of Israel, a country whose name means 'the white' in Arabic because of its snow-capped mountains. Lebanon is divided between Christian and Muslim communities and has a history of civil war and invasion. For all that, it is very historic, with lots of character packed into a small space.

Also in the pipeline are *A Maverick Australian Way, A Maverick Asian Way* and *A Maverick Pacific Way.*

See Mary Jane's books and blog on a-maverick.com

MARY JANE WALKER

How to see images from this book in colour and at higher resolution

You can view the images in this book in colour on a Kindle Fire or on a tablet or computer screen with a Kindle app.

For higher resolution images, go to the front page of my website **https://www.a-maverick.com.**

In a part of the front page that is about *Iran: Make Love not War,* you will see this button, once the preview has been uploaded:

Preview with Colour Images

Click it to view the preview, which omits much text and some of the black and white photographs but contains all the colour images in the book along with some of the black and white images.

MARY JANE WALKER

Contents

IRAN: MAKE LOVE NOT WAR

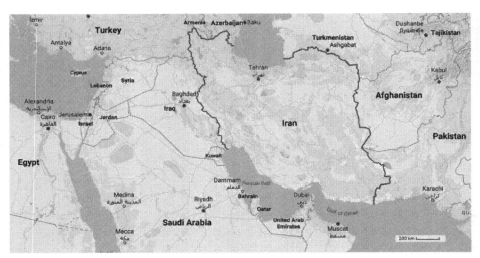

Iran in the World. *Map data ©2019 GeoBasis-DE/BKG (©2009), Google, MapaGISrael, ORION-ME. Iranian land borders marked out in red for this book.*

Introduction

AFTER trying to climb Mount Ararat in Eastern Turkey (which is a whole other story, documented on my website and blog a-maverick.com!), I crossed the border into nearby Iran, or Persia: a fabled land that I'd long wanted to visit, whatever its current unpopularity in the West.

I ended up spending three weeks in Iran, in the September and October of 2018; and I've got lots of amazing photos to share with you, along with videos that appear in some blog posts I've put up about Iran, as well.

But first, why go there in the first place? I'll run through some of the things that are distinctive about Iran; setting the scene for my own accounts of travel a bit further on.

I read a blog about how to travel from Turkey to Tehran overland; and it inspired me to give it a go.

This is the route I followed, starting from the Turkish border-region town of Doğubeyazıt, close to Mount Ararat, and then on to the capital of Tehran and down south through the middle of the country. I'll be describing my itinerary in more detail in Chapter 2, below.

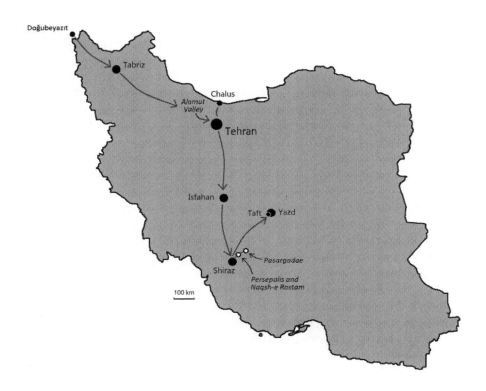

While I was in Iran, I would also see smugglers, prostitutes working under the cover of a custom called temporary marriage (sanctioned by clerics) and be offered beer and all the drugs under the sun.

A cigarette smuggler on the Turkish-Iranian border, stuffing cigarettes down his trousers

I also learned about how the culture of the nation is not merely the 'official' one, but also one that has been shaped by its love of art and by the satirical quality of its most famous poets, who used their wit against arbitrary authority, religion carried to tiresome excess, and anyone who uses, abuses or bullies others.

I also discovered that in ethnic-minority regions in the north, the writ of the government hardly ran and that many people did what they liked.

It wasn't like what you read in the Western media about Iran as this buttoned-down sort of a place: almost the opposite.

CHAPTER 1

Iran Travel Tips

THE main airport for international air arrivals is Tehran. But because of international sanctions and embargoes, there are only a limited range of airlines flying in and out of Tehran. English-speaking and East Asian countries do not serve Iran. The only large Western airlines that fly to Tehran at the moment are Lufthansa and Alitalia.

Russian, Ukrainian, Turkish, Indian and Middle Eastern airliners are more likely to be seen in Tehran, including those of major international carriers like Emirates, Qatar Airways and Air India.

If you travel to Iran and get an Iranian stamp on your passport you may not be allowed to enter the United Sates. For that reason, the Iranians will often give you a visa stamped on a separate piece of paper.

TripAdvisor works well in Iran for accommodation and things to do. There are many hostels that cater for international tourists on a budget.

Western banking sanctions mean that you cannot use an ordinary credit card anywhere in Iran. Instead, it's necessary to get a local debit card called a Mah Card, and to put money on that (refundable when you leave the country, if there is a positive balance). This can be organised online before you get to Iran, with a topped-up Mah Card delivered to your accommodation when you get there.

I was able to use Express VPN for ten dollars a month, which is necessary if you want to post on Facebook while in Iran. You can also use Whatsapp in Iran without any problems.

I was going to enter Iran on my British passport because I use my New Zealand passport most of the time. I always travel with my NZ passport and I was going to be going to several of the countries that are offside with Iran on my NZ passport. I thought it would be prudent to use my British passport for Iran, and the NZ passport for the other countries.

It turned out that I'd got things the wrong way around. New Zealand has no particular quarrel with Iran. But Britain is one of the countries that are always offside. The Brits have just arrested an Iranian freighter at Gibraltar, after all. And if there were to be a war between Iran and the Americans, the British would probably join in on the American side.

It turns out that at the time, if I went as a British tourist, I would have had to take a formal guided tour in a group of at least two, plus guide. There's a useful and up-to-date blog on these sorts of travel details, called Borders of Adventure.

But before all that fully dawned on me, I paid some money upfront to a travel agent in London. This was a waste because it locked me, as a solo traveller, into a busload-of-Brits package-tour thing, which I became less and less keen on the more I researched it online. I looked at all the guided tours for British people and found that I would have had to shell out a lot of money to get to all the places I wanted to go to. Plus, not having the freedom to wander off and do my own thing.

Plus, it was hard to even get a visa on a British passport! I'd applied in January, and after ringing this guy in London about forty times by the time July rolled round, I still didn't have a visa yet!

I was getting really, really anxious because by July I was in the Middle East already and facing the prospect of using up my travel time and having to go home without ever having got a visa for Iran. I felt that my Middle East trip would be incomplete if I couldn't get into Iran. That magical, mysterious, and, as it now seemed, quite inaccessible land of mystery!

Eventually he said to me, "look, just use your Kiwi passport and it won't be a problem." Hallelujah! I wish I'd known that six months before.

And so, I applied for a visa on my New Zealand passport in Istanbul. This took only three or four days to go through. The Iranians interviewed me and didn't seem put out by the fact that my New Zealand passport was full of American and Israeli stamps. In fact, I could have got a visa from the Iranian embassy in Wellington before I left! The Iranians give you a stamp on a piece of paper that you can use to get into Iran. Because it's on a separate piece of paper you don't have to show the Americans or anyone else who might bar you from entering their country because you've been to Iran.

It's worth keeping abreast of all these blacklists, especially in the age of President Trump, who some time back issued (tweeted?) a whole list of allegedly terrorist-filled countries that you wouldn't be able get into the USA from, anymore. The list included Iran, and Lebanon too.

So, the British visa thing was a six-month nightmare that I could have completely avoided.

On the other hand, you could physically do Iran by yourself. I met women who were travelling alone in Iran: it's a very safe place. If a woman is attacked or raped the perpetrator runs the risk of being hanged, especially if the woman is a foreign visitor. So, I suppose, thinking that you could be hanged would put a lot of people off raping foreign women. That's sort of the rule.

I stayed in hostels run by a group called See You in Iran. These offer a choice of own rooms or dorm rooms and have several hostels in various cities.

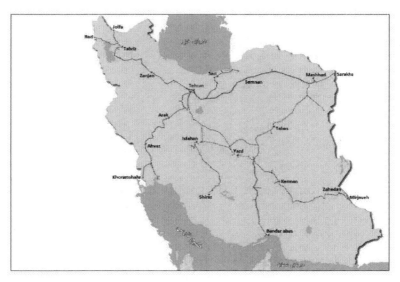

Iranian Railway system in 2014, Image by Navid22, CC-BY-SA 4.0 via Wikimedia Commons

Iran has quite an extensive network of railways, which runs to all the major cities and carries many passenger services. There are also very comfortable inter-city coach services. Fares are quite cheap by Western standards.

There will soon be a high-speed rail line from Tehran to Isfahan, via Qom. This will surely be a bit more expensive than the regular services!

CHAPTER 2

Where I Went

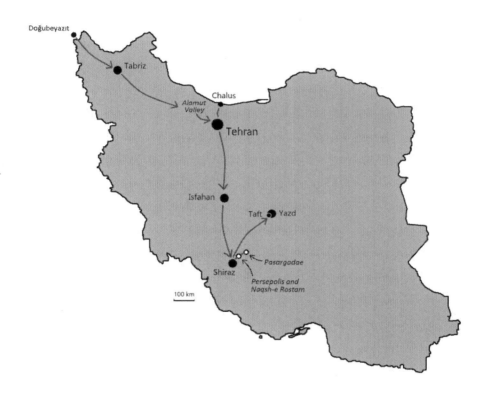

I first visited the north-western city of Tabriz, where I got properly organised for the trip. And then I went on to the Alamut Valley, once home to a guild of Mediaeval assassins:

11

rebels fighting for the poor and downtrodden more or less, whose targets were the local equivalents of the Sheriff of Nottingham at the time. Their leader, Hassan-i Sabbah, dwelt on a spectacular crag. His castle is now being restored.

A romantic portrayal of Hassan-i Sabbah. Public domain image via Wikimedia Commons.

From Alamut, I went on to Tehran, the capital of Iran, with its many attractions such as the fabulous Golestan ('Rose Garden') Palace.

The Golestan Palace: Hall of Mirrors

From Tehran, I took a side trip to the Caspian Sea resort of Chalus. The land of Iran is sandwiched between the Persian Gulf to the south and the Caspian Sea to the north. In spite of its name, the Caspian Sea is actually a lake. It's the world's biggest lake, in fact: one and a half times as big as all of North America's Great Lakes put together! Because it's so big, and also because it's slightly salty, it's not called a lake but rather, the Caspian Sea.

The Caspian Sea. NASA *public domain image (MODIS image from the Terra satellite, 11 June 2003), via Wikimedia Commons.*

The southern shores of the Caspian Sea, looking northward. Three of the roads through the mountains, on the right, can be seen converging on Tehran which is just off the photo's edge to the south. Photo by NASA astronaut Scott Kelly, taken from the International Space Station on 27 July 2015. Public domain image, via NASA and Wikimedia Commons.

The Caspian Sea's Iranian shore lies just north of a belt of mountains and green forests, which the mountains help to sustain by catching moisture from the Caspian Sea as mist and rain. About six million people live between the sea and the woodlands on a sort of riviera, which stretches for four hundred kilometres along the shore and can be seen from space, as somewhere that's lit-up at night.

The Caspian riviera is where people from Tehran go on holiday. The great forest, which adds to the area's attractions, was declared a UNESCO World Heritage site on 5 July, 2019: the latest in what's already a long list of World Heritage sites in Iran.

You can see the mountains, which are called the Alborz, in this photo of myself on a new pedestrian bridge in Tehran. From the city, it's possible to climb to a lookout in the Alborz, visit a hillside summer palace complex called Sa'dabad, and even take a gondola up to ski-fields.

On the new Tabiat ('Nature') pedestrian bridge over a motorway trench in Tehran, with another bridge and the city centre in the **background.** *In the far distance is the Alborz mountain range, with the Caspian Sea on the other side.*

It's because of the Alborz, and their forests, that Robin Hood types like Hassan-i Sabbah were able to flourish in this area. Although it's where the capital is now, northern Iran has always had a bit of a wild-frontier reputation. The early civilisation of

Persia was actually based in the south, and the capital was only shifted to Tehran as recently as 1796.

Which is very recent, by the standards of a country so ancient that in 1971 it celebrated the 2,500th anniversary of its foundation.

After Tehran, I went south to the delightful, planned city of Isfahan, perhaps the first 'garden city'. It has a famous boulevard, famous gardens, famous bridges, a famous town square and some of the most amazing mosques and palaces in all of Iran as well.

Alcove of one of the mosques on Naqsh-e Jahan square, Isfahan

Ali Qapu Palace, Naqsh-e Jahan square, Isfahan

Everywhere south of the Caspian Sea and its belt of woodlands is quite dry. Isfahan depends on a river called the Zayandeh to keep it fresh and green.

Unfortunately, the Zayandeh had dried up completely when I was there.

A tourist map showing the Zayandeh river and its green embankment

By the embankment of the dried-up Zayandeh, guarded by a pair of statues of small and not-particularly-fearsome lions

18

21st-century Iran has huge water problems. This is partly because of global warming, and partly because of a combination of population growth and international sanctions that limit food imports, so that more water has to be taken to grow food in the desert.

A big lake west of Tabriz, Lake Urmia, which used to be a hundred and forty kilometres from end to end, has dried up quite dramatically since the early 1980s.

Lake Urmia in 1984. The lake is below its maximum level in this image, as the volcano in the middle has been an island from time to time. NASA *public domain image via Wikimedia Commons.*

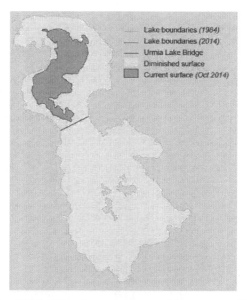

Lake Urmia in 2014. The latest space photos on Google Satellite View show more water than in this map, but the level is still very low. Map by Atila Kagan, CC-BY-SA 4.0 via Wikimedia Commons.

A hundred years ago, Iran's population was only about 10 million. At the time of the Islamic Revolution in 1979, it was about 40 million. Today, it is more than 80 million. In a mostly desert country, such population growth can't help but put pressure on things.

From Isfahan and its dried-up river, apparently now flowing again (but perhaps not for long), I went on to Shiraz, after which a famous wine is named, even though the present Islamic Republic of Iran is 'dry'. It turns out that they were a bit more tolerant in the old days. Shiraz is the home of the famous

20

Mediaeval poets Sa'adi and Hafez, and I visited their tombs. Poets like these are to the Persian language what Shakespeare is to English.

Sa'adi in a Rose Garden. Mughal dynasty image ca. 1645, in the public domain via Wikimedia Commons.

While in Shiraz, I visited the ancient monument sites of Naqsh-e Rostam, where emperors such as Xerxes are buried inside a cliff. You might remember Xerxes as the evil, camped-up villain in the film *300*, all dripping with rings and gold chains. Well, he wasn't really like that.

And I went on to Persepolis, the ancient capital of Persia which was burned by the Greek conqueror Alexander the Great (or not-so-great if you are a Persian). And then to Pasargadae where the tomb of Cyrus the Great, the founder of Persia, still stands.

Here's the Faravahar, ancient symbol of Iran's indigenous Zoroastrian religion, at Persepolis.

The Faravahar, a symbol of the ancient Zoroastrian religion of Iran, at Persepolis

A modern sign at a Zoroastrian centre, in Yazd, explains the significance of the Faravahar, also spelt Frahvahar, said to be the origin of the wedding ring.

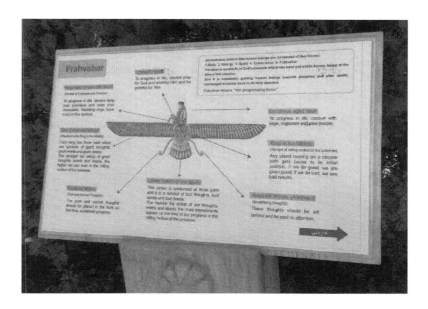

From Shiraz and its nearby ancient sites, I went finally to the incredible desert city of Yazd, where wind-catching towers pull cool, moist air out of caverns to air-condition the people's homes, all without electricity. And to its satellite town of Yazd, also famous for its old quarter.

Windcatcher towers of Yazd

The area around Yazd is also a stronghold of the Zoroastrian religion, now largely displaced by Islam elsewhere in Iran. I visited a Zoroastrian shrine and school and the famous 'towers of silence' where the deceased used to be laid out for vultures to eat, the funeral custom of the Zoroastrians at the time they were built.

Along the way, I took lots of photos and videos of fabulous, sumptuous beauty: mosques, palaces, tapestries, bazaars, and modern art. For, it turns out that Iran is one of the most artistic countries in the world.

CHAPTER 3

Getting across the Border

IT'S about twenty or thirty kilometres from the mountain town of Doğubeyazıt, where I was based for my Mount Ararat adventures, to the border. Here's a map, which shows the route I took and also relation of the area to the Caspian Sea as well as Lake Urmia — the one that has nearly dried up.

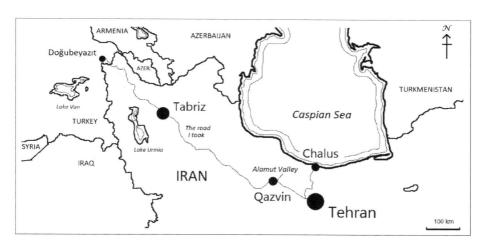

The first stage of my journey into Iran

Like most people in this part of Turkey, my mountain guide, who'd helped me on Ararat, was Kurdish. The nearest bit of Iran was mostly inhabited by Kurds too.

I thought it might help if my guide in Turkey could hook me up with a driver from among his relations on the other side. This person could take me through to Tabriz, my first stop in Iran, and maybe further on if necessary.

Since I'd never been to Iran and had no idea what to expect, I thought that hiring a trustworthy driver would be a really good idea, especially if they could also serve as a local guide. It would cost a lot more than catching buses. But I figured it would be money well spent if it helped save me from getting lost in a bad part of town. My Turkish/Kurdish guide said he did know a few kinsfolk on the other side. So that's what we decided to do.

A friend gave us both a ride to the Turkish customs. I was to change money there and meet my driver on the other side.

I'd heard that I would have to dress appropriately, it being Iran and all that. So, I was wearing a green caftan that I'd bought from Coptic Christians in Egypt, and a black-and-white West Bank Palestinian keffiye, the kind Yasser Arafat wore, for a headscarf. This mix of styles probably made me look very international!

The West Bank is the sort of place where the temperature varies between burning hot and biting cold. My keffiyeh was made of wool, for the cold. But this was September and my head was boiling. I seriously thought about taking it off as soon as the coast was clear, whether I was in Iran or not.

Eventually I made it to the head of the line and spoke to a woman dressed very somberly in a black chador — the Persian word for strict Islamic female attire, and also for 'tent' — and she said it was very safe for women to go to Iran without a guide and that I should have just caught the bus after all. (It was very safe, as things turned out!)

At this point I haven't yet set foot in Iran, beyond the point of talking to a black-clad female border guard. So, I should recap on the trouble I had in trying to get to Iran, actually.

Anyhow, my Turkish/Kurdish guide and I went through customs, and the Turkish official asked if I was a diplomat. And I thought "that's really interesting." Perhaps the international nature of my kaftan and keffieyeh wasn't just a wardrobe muddle! Maybe it really did make me look like some kind of seasoned international traveller.

Outside the customs post, where they asked if I was a diplomat!

27

There wasn't an issue going through the Turkish customs; and then on the Iranian side there wasn't an issue either. Because I was being handed from a Turkish guide to an Iranian driver nobody was worried about what I was doing there by myself, as they might have been otherwise; and I also had sufficient funds to change.

Now, the Iranian money, that was another story. The official unit of currency is called the Rial. Individually, the Rial is almost worthless: I changed a thousand US dollars into 40 million Rials, which gives you an idea of how much one Rial is worth. Or not.

Perhaps for that reason, Iranians like to reckon the price in Tomans, an old currency unit that was worth ten Rials when last officially issued in 1965. The Toman's not been an official currency unit for years, and officially the signs are all supposed to give the price in Rials. Yet the shopkeeper may still quote you the price, verbally, in Tomans. It's not 90% off — just Tomans!

It's good to have both American and local money, really, and you need to keep an eye on your currency. Later on, when I went to Tehran, I discovered the Mah Card that you could put money on. When you left Iran, they would refund your money; and the administration fees were not high at all.

CHAPTER 4

Tabriz and the road of the Martyrs: Mistresses and hash

AT the border, I had no real plan apart from to go to Tabriz. Perhaps I would be driven further. Petrol (gasoline) is very cheap in Iran, so much so that I heard that it was smuggled over the border in spite of all the difficulties and dangers of being a gas-smuggler.

The cheapness of fuel kept the costs of being driven around Iran down to a reasonable level, though it was still costlier than the bus. At least once you'd paid for the car and the driver, filling up the tank wouldn't blow an additional hole in your wallet the way it does in New Zealand.

The first thing we did, very shortly after hitting the road, was to pick up the driver's brother in a border town. He was to be my guide. There, I was confronted with a cigarette smuggling ring. I saw men stuffing cigarettes down their trousers.

They do this at great risk. So much for respectability! I was a bit nervous at being in possession of a thousand American dollars in cash in what seemed like bandit country. But they were honourable bandits, and so we carried on, the driver, the driver's brother, and me.

In Tabriz I spent my first night with the driver's wife, mother-in-law and mother. And the very first thing his wife said to me was, "If you don't wear a hijab [headscarf] in Iran you'll be killed."

She didn't speak much English but she just sort of got her finger and put it across her neck and said: "You'll be killed." Hmmm, I thought.

My driver also told me the Revolutionary Guard used to make him remove the rings from his fingers and cut his hair, and said he hated it. He added that they had stopped picking on him lately.

Kurdish money changers at the airport outside Tabriz turned my thousand American dollars into 40 million Rials. That was a whole sack of money. The driver's brother helped with the transaction.

You can't use foreign cards in Iranian ATMs; but you can organise a Mah Card from overseas. And you can put the money in overseas as well. Since I only found out about Mah Cards once I got to Tehran, we were still doing everything the old-fashioned way.

I always get a local SIM when I travel, and I was lucky enough to get one from a store in five minutes, beating the queues, by using my Kurdish guide's name instead of mine.

Everywhere, you saw an official, composite image of the late Imam Khomeini seated cosily in front of his successor as Supreme or holy Leader, Ali Khamein'i (no relation), as Khamein'i looks now.

Before the 1979 revolution, Khomeini was known as the Ayatollah Khomeini: Imam is the most senior and honorary religious title in the Shi'a tradition, an honorific bestowed after the revolution when Khomeini became Iran's first Supreme Leader. In the West we still think of him as the Ayatollah, the title he held when he was getting the most Western press. Khomeini died in 1989 and was succeeded by Khamein'i, who obviously didn't have a white beard back then.

The two Supreme Leaders

So, that was interesting.

And the driving in Iran — yeah, well. The bus service that I was to use was safe and reliable. But private motorists drove fast. Really fast.

In Tabriz, we went sightseeing, my first chance to see Iran. I stayed with an Azeri, the ethnic group most common in neighbouring Azerbaijan. His wife discussed the prostitution that was being practised in Iran by way of temporary marriages, which she objected to. It was the first I'd heard of that!

Later on, I was to meet a woman who explained to me that the custom of temporary marriage also enabled people who didn't actually want to get married right now to have relationships, since premarital sex was technically illegal. She was living with her boyfriend, but they hadn't bothered to get a temporary marriage. She came from a wealthy background and was headstrong. She said the authorities would have to catch her in the act to prove anything!

With my driver outside the Blue Mosque in Tabriz

Tabriz is the capital of an Iranian province called 'East Azerbaijan'. Azeris are a majority here, too. The Azeris are not related to the Persians but rather to the Turks. On the other hand, the Kurds, who straddle the Turkish border, aren't related to the Turks but rather to the Persians. Contested for centuries between old-time Turkish and Persian empires, this region is very mixed and remains so for hundreds of kilometres on either side of the official frontier.

The Kurds don't have an independent country of their own. The reason the Azeris do is because there used to be a region of the former Soviet Union known as Soviet Azerbaijan, on the other side of the Soviet/Iranian border from the Azeri districts of Iran. When the Soviet Union collapsed, the former Soviet Azerbaijan found itself an independent republic. Such are the accidents of history. If there had been a Soviet Kurdistan, it would probably have become independent too. But there wasn't.

Tabriz is full of heritage, and I'm annoyed I didn't spend more time there and take more photos (I've got a lot more for the other cities).

By the way, you can look up the monuments of every city on Wikimedia templates, as well as the usual guides. It's a really good idea.

And there's new stuff as well. We saw an interesting monument and park that had apparently only just been created in an eastern part of Tabriz. The white monument we saw didn't come up on the template for Tabriz, which also makes me think it is new.

An interesting memorial

Iran has had a massive programme of building new houses and parks going for some years. The Iranian government takes the cities very seriously. Partly, this is because Iran has had such a massive population explosion over the last few decades, with just about all of the new population appearing in the cities.

Anyhow, here's a photo of me beside another monument, a statue of the poet Khaqani, who lived in Tabriz in the same general era as Hafez and Sa'adi in Shiraz.

By a statue of Khaqani, another famous Mediaeval poet who lived in Tabriz, at Khaqani Park near the Blue Mosque. Poets are highly esteemed in Iranian culture.

In those days Iranians were few, and the cities were small. And yet they managed to produce one of the world's most amazing cultures, and even a large empire which, though it was frequently conquered by outsiders because Iranians were so few, always bounced back.

35

For the next night I stayed with another local family so as not to impose on my driver's relatives. Airbnb doesn't operate in Iran. Hawkers on the street offered accommodation, though you took your chances there. And there was also social media: Snapchat and Whatsapp.

The Iranian government keeps trying to censor the local Internet and because of that you can't easily use Facebook directly, though I was able to use Express VPN for ten dollars a month. TripAdvisor is widely used in Iran; there's no ban on that.

Word of mouth also seems to convey a lot of information. That was how I got my second place. The man of this new house was a business owner recommended by my driver and his brother; the ones who had been recommended to me by my Kurdish guide in Turkey.

I slept on the floor in the children's room, and the businessman's wife was lovely. You should have seen what they grew. They had a veritable oasis, with plenty of fruit and olives.

The next morning, I was offered some hash by the businessman and I thought, hmmm (once again): this is really interesting, to be offered hash in Iran. And it wasn't the only drug I was offered either. I read a blog that said prostitution was quite common as well.

So, what you get in the international media in terms of Iran being strait-laced, and what you get in terms of actually visiting the country, are two different things.

I guess it was like America during Prohibition. Literally so, for later on I ran into people who seemed to have no problem getting hold of booze, which is officially banned from open sale in the Islamic Republic of Iran as well of course.

So, I wasn't particularly impressed, and I said to both my guide and my driver that I wanted to go to somewhere a bit more authentic and less Westernised. I said that I wanted to go to Alamut, a famous scenic valley with a ruined castle overlooking it, several hundred kilometres further on down the road.

Our growing band of travellers now included the businessman and a further addition. his mistress. We all went in down the road in the direction of the Alamut Valley in the one car. That pissed me off a bit, considering I'd just met the businessman's charming wife, and yet now I had to be nice to his mistress, of whom he was very protective. Bloody hypocrisy! Plus, things were getting a bit crowded by this stage.

Our original plan had been to hit the main road leading south-east to Tehran and then turn left after a short while to Gilan province and Rudkhan Castle, near the border with Azerbaijan, and from there to head for Alamut along the beautiful shores of the Caspian Sea.

But the roads were too bad up there apparently, and it was going to take about two days to get to Alamut Castle that way. So, instead of the scenic route, we just kept on down the main road.

Even on the main road, it was a really long drive. We left at about ten o'clock and were still driving at five o'clock. Still, the drive to Alamut was fantastically interesting.

Gate of Rudkhan Castle on the northern slopes of the Alborz, photo by *Mansour Nasiri (2007), CC-BY-SA 3.0 via Wikimedia Commons*

They had photos of heroes lining the road the entire way. Iran was severely affected by the war with Iraq from 1980 to 1988. Nobody really knows how many people were killed in the war, but the government of Iran admits to losing 184,000 troops on its side. The war was triggered by Saddam Hussein making a grab for Iran's oilfields, which are in the predominantly Arab part in the southwest, close to Basra and also close to Kuwait.

The war ended in utter stalemate and a UN-brokered peace deal that enforced a return to the way things were before. So, it was all for nothing in the end, except insofar as Saddam had been prevented from winning by the Iranians, who got no credit for it from the West.

Image of a martyr on the main road to Tehran

At the time, Iraq was egged on by the same Western powers who would later turn on Saddam. For, in the 1980s, Western governments disliked the Ayatollah Khomeini even more than they disliked Saddam Hussein. Of some relevance here was the fact that the Ayatollah's regime had lately taken the occupants of the American embassy hostage, in the hope of achieving the extradition of the recently-deposed Shah. I'll have a bit more to say about all that further on.

39

Continuing along the road toward Qazvin, where we would soon turn off toward Alamut, we noticed that there was a bit of forest along the way. It wasn't the scenic route, but it was a really interesting journey. Or maybe it was just that I was new to the country.

CHAPTER 5

The Valley of the Assassins and the Freedom of the North: being offered all drugs under the sun and women with no hijabs

THE history of Alamut is fascinating. You may have heard the fabled tale of 'Old Man of the Mountain', which goes like this. Once upon a time, there was an old man who lived in a castle in Persia.

There, he created a guild of Ninja-like assassins, to be sent out into the world to kill corrupt tax collectors and other oppressors of the people. The assassins were fearless and struck in broad daylight in front of vast crowds for maximum effect, heedless of their own safety.

In the more fanciful versions of the tale, the Old Man got his assassins hopelessly befuddled on drugs — hashish, in particular — and led them into a beautiful garden, telling them that this was Paradise and that it was the place to which they would return if they were slain by their target's bodyguards.

The story of the Old Man of the Mountain inspires the modern computer game, Assassin's Creed.

Amazingly, it's true; though probably not the vision-of-Paradise bit, which seems to have been added later on by Marco Polo and other travellers who heard about the whole business third or fourth-hand.

The Old Man of the Mountain was an Isma'ili religious leader and warrior named Hassan-i Sabbah. (The Isma'ili are a sect of Shi'a Islam not seen as heretical, unlike the Baha'i.)

Hassan-i Sabbah, who lived from around 1050 to 1124 CE (AD), directed most of his energies not only against particular officials but also against the country's recent conquerors.

Strategists commenting on the present Gulf crisis often say that Iran is unconquerable, with its mountains and vast distances (the country is several times bigger than France).

Well, whether that's true or not today, Iran has certainly been conquered many times in the past. Perhaps that's because, until recently, this vast and cultured country held only a surprisingly small population.

In Hassan-i Sabbah's time, Iran was ruled from Baghdad, at that time a Turkish rather than an Arab capital. Baghdad's a long way away from northern Iran, and so Hassan-i Sabbah decided to fight not only particular injustices, but also to fight the Turks in a wider sense. He was thus not only a sort of Robin Hood but also a sort of William Wallace, the Scottish independence fighter celebrated in the film *Braveheart*.

Of course, to the Turks, Hassan-i Sabbah and his followers were terrorists. And perhaps his methods were misguided. For, while it has been conquered many times, Iran has always risen again, for reasons that have less to do with its warlike capacities than with the 'soft power' of its culture, which over the centuries has successfully converted Mongols, Turks and Arabs to the Persian way of doing things.

(Hold that thought, for I'm going to come back to it later.)

Anyhow, where does the word assassin come from, and what does it mean? Many people say that it must have something to do with all that hashish.

Well, no. Hassan-i Sabbah called his warriors *Asāsiyyūn*, meaning 'people who are faithful to the foundation': the foundation of the Muslim faith that is, which includes a certain sympathy for the underdog.

But Marco Polo misheard this expression and thought it meant 'people doped up on hashish'! And that seems to be where the story of the fake Paradise crept in.

The Alamut Valley, with cliffs overlooking. This is south of the wettest parts of the Alborz.

Alamut Castle was Hassan-i Sabbah's stronghold. It sits on top of an amazing crag at more than 2,000 metres elevation in the Alamut Valley, an important scenic area in its own right. Alamut means 'the eagle's nest'.

Alamut Cultural Landscape

In the year 1090 A.D Hasan Sabbah, the leader of Ismailites in Ira
chose the Alamut region, as his headquarter for campaign, preachi

You can't see much of the Alamut Castle in this view of its crag,
partly because it's on the other side and partly because it's also quite ruined. You can
see steps at left, for scale.

45

Quite randomly, I found a place to stay on a winding side road leading up to the Alamut Valley and ultimately to the Caspian Sea. We just looked around. We hadn't pre-booked anything. I found this place which had obviously shone in earlier days. It was a bit run down now. But the woman managing it was glad to see us, and she would make us local food.

I had my own room, and the guys shared a room, and the man and mistress left. There were a whole lot of Iranians there, and the women weren't wearing any hijabs, that is, headscarves. They were young Iranian women who said that they didn't want to wear the bloody hijab, and certainly didn't want to get married!

And I met an Iranian guide who asked me what sort of drugs I wanted. That was weird, and I said I didn't want any.

What I found out later was that in this highland area, Hassan-i Sabbah's old stomping ground, there's an unofficial agreement with the leadership that people who go up into the hills can do what they want.

The women there just wore very, very skinny headbands around their heads. They actually don't wear hijabs. They wear tight-fitting clothes, dresses and skirts. And they certainly don't wear the chador ('tent').

And so, I was actually rather shocked to say the least. You get a certain impression of Iran through the media, and it's just not that way at all. Or not everywhere at any rate.

We went up and we had a look at the castle, and it was absolutely beautiful. It wasn't a major climb, and I met an archaeologist and a teacher. At the time I was very fascinated with the Isma'ili sect. I had just been to Egypt and had made a visit to an Isma'ili shrine created by the Aga Khan, the leader of the sect. The castle was being reconstructed by Iran's Cultural Heritage Organisation, and a mosque was being built as well.

We wandered about the site, but couldn't really go in. We had to hike up a hill to get to the castle, the 'Mountain' in other words, and at the top there was a person selling tea. I asked for coffee at first! There were forty varieties of tea on sale, some of them quite amazing!

In the amazing Alamut Canyon

47

Looking the other way in the Alamut Canyon

The castle was being restored; there wasn't much of the original castle left, to be honest

Anyone for tea?

Me, my guide, and tea

I got to chatting with some of the locals who lived in the area; and they started singing Kurdish songs. I heard so many Kurdish

49

songs. Many of the Kurdish songs were songs of warriors. There were a lot of women fighting in for the cause of Kurdish autonomy in eastern Syrian autonomy where it borders Iran, in a left-wing organisation called the YPJ, left-wing as you can sort of tell from the red star in the flag. And the women I met just literally sang these amazing war-ballads, like WWII partisans.

Flag of the YPJ. Public domain image via Wikimedia Commons.

It was a surprise to meet Kurds so close to Tehran.

In fact, the highlands of the Alborz are a Kurdish stronghold, one that is admittedly a long way from most of the other centres of Kurdish population. That's probably another reason why the writ of the authorities doesn't seem to run all that firmly here.

Reading more about the Kurds, I discovered that there are several different Kurdish groups whose languages, or dialects, can differ from each other almost as much as English and German; and are written in different scripts as well. The fact that the Kurds aren't *totally* united is a product of the fact that they have lived for centuries under several different foreign rulers; who probably do everything they can to sustain this disunity.

Personally, I had no real opinion about Kurdish politics, other than that they should have been given a country of their own at some stage. There are just as many Kurds in the world as there are Canadians. And yet every single one of them lives in someone else's country.

As it turned out my driver's brother was a commander in the Kurdish army fighting the Iranians.

.

CHAPTER 6

Chalus: Prostitutes and beer on the Caspian Riviera

IT was really hot and the mountains were semi-arid; we weren't quite yet in the coastal climate belt, at Alamut. People who lived in the valley actually went into a nearby village to get clean water!

But at last we were bound for this curious inland sea, which has such a moderating influence on the local environment, and to its cool coastal forests.

(When Europeans first came to Australia, they hoped that they would find something like the Caspian Sea in the interior of the red continent. Well, they didn't. Not unless you count Lake Eyre, which is more like Lake Urmia and even more inclined to dry up completely.)

In theory we could have driven on to the Caspian Sea over local roads; but there was a good chance that they would peter out at some point into tracks that our car wouldn't be able to handle.

The most reliable way to get to the Caspian Sea was to go back the way we'd come till we were on the main road again, head south-east to Tehran for a while, and then turn left onto a good road heading directly northward to the seaside resort of Chalus.

On the beach at Chalus

In Chalus, we soon found a good place to stay. We went out for a walk, and next thing I was offered a beer. You can imagine my surprise. This guy comes out of a shop and goes, "do you want some beer?" My driver and his brother were all up for it, though I wasn't. We walked further down the road, and there was a whole group of drunk people dancing in a pub.

And I was actually really really shocked (or surprised), for I had never imagined that in Iran people would be drinking, let alone dancing conspicuously. Later, my driver said, "oh, do you want to go into the pub?" And I said no, for if you want to do that in 'dry' Muslim' country that's a real issue.

I assumed that if I got caught up in this I would get into trouble and I would not be interested in that.

But since the authorities have to arrest *somebody*, they will probably arrest whoever it is they don't know. And if you are a visitor, well then, as the safety posters always used to say, 'This Means You'.

And we also saw a lot of prostitutes further along the coast, too.

I didn't go swimming, as I didn't have one of those rather all-covering Islamic swimming costumes (so there's something else to pack for an Iran holiday, by the way).

We went to restaurants and had delicious fresh fish and vegetables. The next day we had a traditional breakfast. There were very unusual dishes that I tried: I wish I could remember what they were. I talk about Iranian food a bit later on. So maybe I'll describe what we had, after all!

We travelled through a river gorge on the way back to Tehran; another fun place to hang out. People were more than willing to say hello and be sociable.

The river gorge

Everyone was friendly and seemed to speak English

CHAPTER 7

History, if you want it

IRAN is the name its people call a country that was known in English, until the 1930s, as Persia: a country quite distinct from the Arab lands, and also from Turkey.

Iran, or Persia, was founded just over two and a half thousand years ago by a charismatic first emperor, Cyrus the Great, whose tomb still survives near the country's ancient ceremonial capital at Persepolis, a site Cyrus may have chosen.

Eagle-Griffon Capital on top of a pillar at Persepolis, the ancient capital of Persia around 550–330 BCE. *This probably bore a wooden beam on top, till the Greeks set fire to it.*

The name Persepolis comes from the surrounding region, the heartland of old-time Iran, a district known as Parsa in the time of Cyrus.

Persepolis is a Greek name which has since been adopted even in Iran, meaning Parsa City.

It's from Parsa that the name Persia has evolved; though ironically enough the Iranians mainly use that name to denote the province of Parsa, or Persia, and not the whole country. It seems that the country as a whole has been known as Iran to its inhabitants for as long as it has existed. For nearly the whole of this time, outsiders kept calling it Persia. Only in the 1930s did the Shah of the time manage to persuade foreigners to start calling it Iran as well.

The word Persian is still used outside Iran to describe all aspects of Iranian culture and history including the country's official, national, spoken and written language.

Although they have similar styles of writing, Persian and Arabic aren't related. Instead, Persian belongs to the same family as many European and Indian languages. Quite a few everyday words in Persian resemble their English equivalents; words like barader ('brother') and dokhtar ('daughter'). This isn't true of Arabic.

So, unlike neighbouring Iraq, Iran isn't an Arab country overall. But there has always been a large Arab minority in modern Iran and historical Persia. And Arabic also has a special religious significance in Iran as the language of the Koran.

Along with Greece and Armenia, Iran is one of only a handful of countries known in the biblical world that still exist on the same spot and speaking pretty much the same language.

Throughout its history, Iran has regularly been invaded and conquered by Arabs, Turks and others. But, just as often, it spread its culture outward into neighbouring lands, partly by means of the sword — as in, Persian Empire — but also by example.

Many neighbouring peoples were nomadic horse-warriors originally: people such as the Turks, the Arabs and the feared Mongols. Such peoples didn't have any urban or metropolitan culture of their own. When they did settle down, they tended to look to Persia for guidance on how to build cities, mosques, and all the other refinements of civilisation.

The countries that surround Iran generally have names that end in -stan. This is a Persian suffix meaning 'here are' or 'land of', so that Uzbekistan is the land of the Uzbeks, and Pakistan the land of the Pure.

Country names ending in -stan are the most obvious trace of a past Persian influence beyond the borders of present-day Iran. But the Persian influence is massive even in countries whose names don't end in -stan, such as the Arab countries, Turkey and India.

A good example of long-distance Persian influence is the Taj Mahal, built in the Persian style by Jahan, an Indian ruler who called himself Shah, the Persian word for king: Shah Jahan.

Basically, Persia was the Greece of the Middle East; a land whose cultural influence extended very far beyond its usual borders, and also helped to carry it through the times when it was, itself, invaded and occupied by others.

Where did that culture come from? Well, oddly enough, some say that it came from carpet-weaving: a skill for which the Persians are famous. The words 'Persian' and 'carpet' go together in the same way as 'French' and 'cuisine'.

A carpet-seller in Shiraz

In fact, the association between Persians and carpet is more longstanding. The oldest surviving carpet in the world, the Pazyryk Carpet, was woven by the Scythians, a sister-people of the Persians, sometime around 400 BCE. It's already quite a sophisticated product; in ways that imply that the Persians were already weaving Persian carpets in the time of Cyrus the Great.

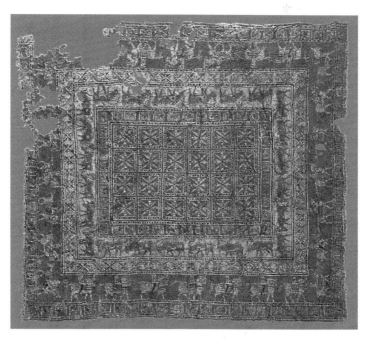

The Pazyryk Carpet, ca. 400 BCE. Public domain image via Wikimedia Commons.

Carpet-weaving, with ever-more ingenious patterns, may have helped to create a culture that looked positively on innovation, mathematics, and the search for patterns in nature and society, rather than on force like the Spartans.

Persia also lay on the Silk Road, between the Mediterranean and Chinese worlds. Whatever new designs of luxurious textiles that it came up with, in lighter fabrics, could be traded and exported.

Textile designs evolved into fantastic forms of architecture and a general love of beauty and mathematics; two things that are more closely related than is generally realised.

Geometrical Architecture in Shiraz

'Cubic equation and intersection of conic sections', page from a thesis by Omar Khayyam (1048–1131), held in Tehran University.
Public domain image via Wikimedia Commons.

There's a very interesting web-page called 'Heirloom Tech', which describes some of the stunning mathematical-cum-artistic achievements of Persian and Islamic culture, the one tending to blend into the other in later centuries.

The 'Heirloom Tech' of old Persia include a music room with noise-cancelling acoustics of a kind that you'd need a computer to design nowadays, all done hundreds and hundreds of years ago.

That all these were hallmarks of the culture of the Persians was something that would often be said.

Another invention of the Persians was monotheism, in the sense that it appears in Judaism, Christendom and Islam. That is to say, a god of light who battles the forces of darkness, as opposed to the sorts of religions where there were lots of gods and goddesses quarrelling with one another in a universe that was a bit more random.

Monotheism, in this sense, first appeared in the form of the Persian indigenous religion of Zoroastrianism (though one Egyptian Pharaoh had also, earlier, attempted to elevate the sun-god to supreme status). Founded by the prophet Zoroaster, or more correctly, Zarathustra, Zoroastrianism directly influenced the Jewish faith, and from there, Christianity and Islam.

This is recognised by the Islamic Republic, which extends toleration to Zoroastrians, followers of the Jewish faith, and Christians, on the grounds that their prophets are all recognised as forebears of Muhammad.

Zoroaster, or Zarathustra, as he is conventionally represented

And here's one last thought on the durability of Persian culture. The tomb of Cyrus the Great, who founded the Persian empire in the time of the Spartans and the Athenians, still exists. It's said to have once borne an inscription in which Cyrus asks visitors from the inconceivable future, such as myself, not to begrudge a man who was once the king of a vast realm the small patch of earth he now occupies.

All in all, like many Old World countries, Iran possesses a strong sense of its own historical past and a 'slow culture', as opposed to an impatient one.

CHAPTER 8

The Humiliation of Persia

THAT Persian or Iranian national identity is so deeply bound up with intellectualism, love of beauty and 'soft power' has led, in the past, to a humiliating calumny known as Orientalism or, more specifically, the 'Persian Fallacy'.

The Persian Fallacy holds that Persian culture, precisely because it is so highly developed in artistic, mathematical, and architectural terms, and very heavily reliant on the projection of soft power, must therefore somehow be decadent and even un-manly, in all the various ways that the character of Xerxes seems to be in *300;* a film likened to Nazi race-propaganda by *Slate* critic Dana Stevens and the target of mass protest in Iran.

(The 2014 sequel, *300: Rise of Empire,* was even more bigoted. And it wasn't as if the makers of the series didn't realise it would be controversial, anymore. I suppose their only excuse was that, having created such an over-the-top 'campy villain', they couldn't let their Xerxes character go to waste.)

It was the ancient Greeks, frequently at war with the Persians, who first came up with the Persian Fallacy. Thereafter, it seems to have persisted among the Romans and the Arabs, who often contrasted idealised warrior cultures to those who were soft and citified.

Then, after the passage of many centuries, the fallacy sprang up anew the nineteenth century, when countries such as Persia, indeed pretty much the rest of the world, suddenly fell behind America and Western Europe in industrial terms. The gap had been much closer in the 1700s, but by the later part of the 1800s, countries such as Persia were likely to be judged as 'backward' in spite of their past achievements.

Why were the Persians and those in their sphere of cultural influence industrially backward? Was it just that they were still living in the eighteenth century, but would soon catch up? Or was it because because they were soft and decadent, as the Greeks had said.

In spite of the fact that the first explanation was more plausible, Westerners of the Victorian era often preferred the second. The charge of decadence wasn't applied to the most austere desert Arabs or the Islamic mountain warriors battling it out with Kipling's redcoats near the Khyber Pass, adversaries the Victorians rather admired.

But it was held to be true of the majority of Turks, Persians, and inhabitants of Middle Eastern cities such as Cairo, who were portrayed as lolling round on cushions all day long and smoking hubbly-bubbly pipes, probably laced with hashish, while Westerners got on with progress.

The Victorian revival of the idea that the Persians and their wider cultural realm are decadent is the version that most often goes by the name of Orientalism. Nineteenth-century Orientalism included a whole genre of paintings that tended to fit the stereotype, in ways that ranged from the comparatively mild such as Ernst Rudolf's 'Smoking the Hookah', to stuff that's quite a bit more lurid such as the painting that appears on the cover of the first edition of Edward Said's 1978 book, *Orientalism*. There was a great fondness for paintings of harems and naked white girls being sold as slaves in bazaars; images that are probably more shocking to us now than they were to the Victorians, though for different reasons.

***Ernst Rudolf, 'Smoking the Hookah', public domain image via
Wikimedia Commons***

It wasn't just Westerners who believed in the Persian Fallacy. It was always present in the Middle East, and influenced the thinking of Middle Eastern reformers, who often came to see their own countries as rotten to the point of being in need of a complete cultural makeover. Reformers like Mustafa Kemal Atatürk in Turkey, and the very similar figure of Reza Khan in early twentieth century Persia, sought to modernise and industrialise their countries — which had to be done — and, going further, to Westernise them and suppress many elements of the indigenous culture.

Reza Khan. Public domain image.

Such people were often stern military officers, dressed — of course — in Western-style uniforms.

Persia's humiliations continued in the first half of the twentieth century, when a country still underpopulated, and barely industrialised, was invaded by more modern powers in both World Wars.

In World War One, the Ottoman Turks and the Russians clashed over who was to pluck Tabriz from the carcass of Persia. Only the defeat of the Ottoman Empire and revolution in Russia, which had previously taken other provinces from Persia (notably, Azerbaijan) kept the Tabriz area Persian.

In World War Two, Iran was invaded and taken over by Britain and the Soviet Union, the better to establish a supply corridor from the Persian Gulf to the Caspian Sea. Vitally-needed war materials would be railed up through Iran to Caspian Sea freighters and shipped and barged up the Volga River which pours into the Caspian's northern end, past the crucial choke-point of Stalingrad. The Nazi war machine tried to take Stalingrad in order to choke off the flow of supplies, but failed.

Fair use image, via Wikimedia Commons.

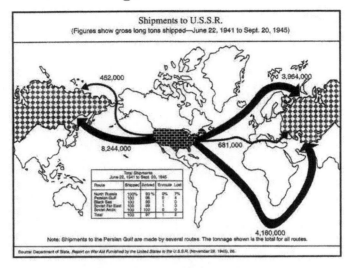

Total World War II US wartime aid shipments to the Soviet Union.
US State Department via Wikimedia Commons, public domain image.

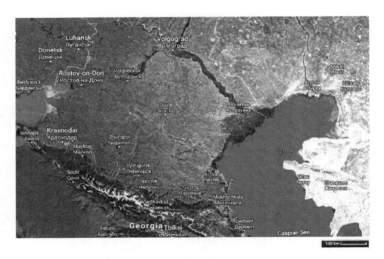

The location of Stalingrad, renamed Volgograd, north-west of the Caspian Sea. *Imagery ©2019 Google, Landsat/Copernicus, Data SIO, NOAA, U.S. Navy, NGA, GEBCO. Map data ©2019 Google.*

And so, history was made; yet from an Iranian point of view, it was being made without their participation.

During World War II the allies had removed Reza Khan from the Iranian throne (he had become Shah in 1925) and installed his son, the last Shah as it would turn out, instead. After the War, the British and the Americans encouraged the Soviets to leave Iran (at first, they weren't going to). Grateful for this, and fearing that he might be removed like his father if he didn't play ball, the Shah then stood by while his nationalist, democratically elected Prime Minister Mohammed Mossaddegh was overthrown in a 1953 coup assisted by the British and the Americans.

As a result, the last Shah came to be seen as a Western puppet, his own plans for the modernisation and Westernisation of Iran less and less acceptable, till he was overthrown and replaced by a clerical regime.

Yet even the rulers of the contemporary Islamic Republic, though clad in flowing robes and turbans, also seem Orientalist or anti-Persian in the sense of rejecting the more liberal aspects of Persian culture and many of the sources of its soft power, in favour of a hard, martial edge.

The martial and defensive attitudes of present-day Iran, though understandable up to a point, have led to conflict with neighbouring powers. Most seriously, Iran and Saudi Arabia have been at daggers drawn, in spite of long-term Persian influences on Arabia which are nearly as important as the Persian influence on Turkey.

A recruiting poster I saw in Shiraz

The origin of this feud seems to have less to do with religious and cultural differences — more on that in the next section — than on the fact that the American-backed Saudi royal family see the current Iranian regime as exporting revolution and the overthrown of wobbly, American-backed monarchies; for which the Iranian Ayatollahs do seem to have a particular antipathy.

76

In other words, so the Saudis believe, it will be a case of the Shah first, the House of Saud next, if the Iranian Islamic Republic is allowed to have its wider way. On the other hand, Turkey, a republic these days and not so obviously beholden to the USA, has fewer problems with Iran right now.

CHAPTER 9

The Several Religions of the Islamic Republic

ALTHOUGH Iran is currently styled as an Islamic Republic, not everyone is a Muslim. There are three significant religious minorities that enjoy a degree of constitutional toleration — Zoroastrian, Jewish and Christian — and one that does not, namely, the Baha'i.

Eternal flame in a Zoroastrian temple in Yazd

Zoroastrianism arose in Persia before the time of Cyrus the Great. A little over a thousand years later, Persian was then taken over by early Arab Muslims. The country was mostly converted to the Muslim religion as a result, though many Zoroastrian customs survive, even among the Muslims, whose religion also recognises Zoroaster, or Zarathustra, as a prophet.

Zoroastrian customs still widely practiced in Iran include a midwinter festival of light called Yalda. Another important Zoroastrian tradition, borrowed likewise by almost everyone, is the idea of the eternal flame as the symbol of anything solemn and reverent. And, of course, the wedding ring.

The Zoroastrian religion influenced the Jews, Christians and Muslims both in terms of customs and festivals, and also in terms of the very idea of a more abstract sort of religion. Nor did it die out in favour of its successors. For there are still many people who practice the Zoroastrian religion.

Zoroastrians are a constitutionally recognised religious minority in Iran, along with Christians and those who practice the Jewish religion.

The three official minorities are partly exempt from the laws of the Islamic Republic. For instance, though alcohol is legally forbidden to Muslims in Iran right now, members of the three minorities are allowed to make wine for consumption within their own communities, so long as they don't sell it to Muslims.

Within Islam there are two main forms, Shi'a and Sunni. For centuries, Persia has mostly practiced Shi'a Islam, as opposed to the Sunni Islam that is more common in the Arab world today. Of the two, Shi'a Islam has a more formal religious hierarchy. Shi'a are also more likely to make use of colourful decoration as a way of inspiring the faithful, in ways that mix geometrical patterns and images from nature with images of angels, saint-like figures (*pir*), Jesus, and even the Virgin Mary — whose quite similar significance in Islam often comes as a surprise to Westerners.

The Archangel Gabriel (with a halo, and flames inside) announcing to a blue-clad Virgin Mary that she is pregnant with Jesus, from a Persian Muslim text. Public domain image via Wikimedia Commons.

Angels on the exterior of Golestan Palace, Tehran, on either side of the long-term symbol of historical Persia, the 'lion and sun'. The angels are thus acting as bearers to the symbol of the state.

The Sunni tradition is less keen on graven images and a formal priesthood; and likewise tends, in architecture, to prefer a more sculptural outcome to the elaborate decoration of surfaces. Here's an example of contemporary architecture in more of a Sunni style, the Museum of Islamic Art in Doha, Qatar.

Though the gulf isn't as wide, the differences between Sunni and Shi'a culture in Islam are often likened to the differences that exist in the Christian world between the cultures of Roman Catholicism and Eastern Orthodoxy on the one hand, and Protestantism on the other.

As I've noted, the three officially-tolerated religious minorities in Iran have certain liberties, and even have reserved seats in the Iranian Parliament. Having said that, there are a couple of important limits to toleration (apart from non-Muslim women still having to wear a headscarf in the street, and so on).

One is that if a non-Muslim converts to Islam, they will inherit all their parents' property if the siblings remain non-Muslim. So, there is a subtle but insistent pressure to convert to Islam for economic reasons.

A black (Ethiopian) Jewish taxi driver was the one who told me first about the skewed inheritance laws. He turned around to me and said, "I'm Jewish, what can I do?"

Secondly, trying to persuade a Muslim to renounce Islam, or for a Muslim to renounce Islam, is treated as a very serious crime and people have actually been executed for such 'apostasy'; though the great majority were left-wing political prisoners in the 1980s.

The Imam Khomeini's notorious 1989 invitation to all Muslims to kill the Indian-born British novelist Salman Rushdie, who comes from a Muslim family, was also inspired by the view that Rushdie was an apostate. This was because of some made-up things that Rushdie had had the Archangel Gabriel say in his 1988 novel, *The Satanic Verses*. Rushdie thought that the Imam was drawing a long bow, but had to go into hiding all the same.

Other religions don't enjoy the limited toleration extended to Christians, Jews and Zoroastrians in Iran. The religious minority that seems to suffer most from official *non*-tolerance is the Baha'i faith. And that's in spite of the fact that, like Zoroastrianism, the Baha'i faith also originated locally, and actually has several hundred thousand adherents in modern Iran.

The Baha'i faith was founded in the nineteenth century by a young merchant from Shiraz, who claimed, at the age of 24, to be a messenger from God, meaning that he was of similar significance to Jesus and Muhammad. Henceforth, he was to be called the Bab.

The Bab was a sort of Muslim equivalent of Joseph Smith: the American who had founded the church of Latter Day Saints, or Mormons, after a similar revelation a few years before.

To this day, Baha'i remain unpopular in the Muslim world in general. Within Iran itself, the Baha'i had the additional problem that the Bab had called for the abolition of the Shi'a clergy, a pillar of the Persian / Iranian state.

At the Jesus-like age of thirty the Bab was executed by the Shah, who had found his utterances treasonable. This followed a debate over the question of whether the Bab should be shown mercy on the grounds of being insane. Either judgement would have suited the Shah's political purposes, I suspect.

Following a century or so of grumbling persecution under a succession of Shahs, Baha'i fortunes actually took a turn for the worse after the Shi'a clergy became the supreme leaders of the state in 1979. These days, Baha'i houses of worship are liable to be demolished; the congregation's access to good jobs and higher education is restricted; and Baha'i are also at risk of being accused of some kind of treason once more if they become too outspoken, just like the Bab.

At the present time, Iran has democratic institutions, but it is still a 'guided democracy' in the sense that the president and the parliament quite literally play second fiddle to the Supreme (clerical) Leader and his paramilitary force.

The Supreme Leader's paramilitaries, more than a hundred thousand strong, are commonly known as the Sepah or Pasdaran in Iran, and as the IRGC in English. This is short for either the Iranian or the Islamic Revolutionary Guard Corps, depending on your preference. The Americans have just declared it a terrorist organisation.

The Islamic regime has a preoccupation with neatness that reminded me of Singapore. In Tabriz, I saw people picking up cigarette butts off the street with sticky tape. Likewise, this 'Don't Smoke' message on a spotless public square in Tehran.

Within Iran, a branch of the IRGC called the Basij takes care of a variety of public order issues to do with being neat, tidy and proper. Ironically enough, this is almost the opposite of the function that the Basij once had. During the Iran-Iraq war of the 1980s, the Basij were the ones who assaulted Iraqi positions head-on in mass waves wearing kamikaze headbands, sometimes over minefields.

Fighter in the Iran-Iraq war, from a museum in Yazd

These days, my driver told me, the Basij would take the rings off his fingers if they noticed them in the street. Men weren't allowed to wear rings. And they would also make him cut his hair.

Another time, I was out walking with a woman with a see-through headscarf and filmy trousers and we suddenly saw some

Basij on a bridge, who would have possibly arrested her. She froze, and we turned around and walked away.

So, a lot of what the Basij does now is like what you see in the black and white photos from a hundred years ago, in which some Keystone cop is measuring a woman's bathing costume with a tape measure to make sure it's not too revealing, to the general amusement of onlookers.

Washington DC police officer Bill Norton measuring bathing costumes ca. 1922. Public domain image, US Library of Congress.

It's all a far cry from being a kamikaze for the revolution. And apparently there's a lot of grumbling about how life in the Basij is not what it once was, albeit that it's a lot safer now.

The current democratically elected president Hassan Rouhani, though he is a Muslim clergyman himself, doesn't have the full support of Islamic hard-liners, and seeks support from secular democrats and liberals who have periodically mounted powerful protests against the Islamic regime; notably the Green Movement that opposed Rouhani's hard-line predecessor Mahmoud Ahmedinajad.

The fragility of the Islamic regime is part of the reason that the north, a historically rebellious region with many minorities, is less strictly governed than other parts.

CHAPTER 10

Taken by Tehran: The lion, the sun and Golestan palace

I was dropped off in Iran's capital city, Tehran, by my driver, at a place called the See You in Iran Hostel. We said goodbye, and he headed back to Tabriz.

The name Tehran means 'Hot Locality', a place hot and dry by the standards of the green side of the Alborz. The site has been occupied by a settlement of some kind or other for about eight thousand years, and was occupied by a city important enough, already, to be known to the ancient Greeks and Romans, who called it Rhagae. The city was destroyed several times in the course of invasions by Arabs, tribal Turks, and Mongols of the Genghis Khan era, but like Persia itself, has always bounced back.

Before Tehran became the capital in 1796, Persia seems to have been most often ruled from the south: by the ruling elites of Baghdad (now in Iraq), Isfahan, and Shiraz, and even, in ancient times, Persepolis.

In the late 1700s, the newly-established Qajar dynasty wanted to move the capital far away from established urban elites in the south, and also to keep a closer eye on the north in view of the growing power of Russia.

And so, the heart of the state was moved to an area that probably seemed quite peripheral before. It was almost as if the capital of the United Kingdom had been moved from London to Edinburgh!

Well, Tehran is not peripheral anymore. These days, the total urban area of Tehran has a population of about 15 million. Some of the modern highlights of Tehran include the striking Azadi ('freedom') tower, built under the last Shah at the beginning of the 1970s as part of his commemorations of the 2,500th anniversary of the founding of Persia; the rather less unique Milad Tower, still one of the highest freestanding structures in the world; and the Tabiat ('nature') pedestrian bridge, which joins two parks over the top of a motorway. The chief architect and designer of the Tabiat Bridge is a woman, Leila Araghian; a fact that is perhaps still worthy of note in Iran.

Azadi Tower, photo by 'Hooperag', (2014) CC-BY-SA 3.0, via Wikimedia Commons

Azadi Tower, then known as Shahyad Tower, in Azadi square, 1971.
Photographer unknown, public domain image via Wikimedia Commons.

'Aerial View of Tehran', by Hansueli Krapf (2008), CC-BY-SA 3.0 via
Wikimedia Commons. This is an aerial view, but you can also get a good view from the
tower in this photo, Milad Tower, also known as the Tehran Tower.

The Tabiat Bridge

The Tabiat Bridge, with the sun and cranes in the background

The Tabiat Bridge

Road in a park

Tehran also has many traditional mosques, markets and bazaars, including the fantastic food-markets of the Tajrish Bazaar in northern Tehran, at the foot of the mountains.

The city has quite a number of hotels and hostels as well. If you look at the website for the See You in Iran Hostel, where I stayed for the whole time I was in Tehran, there is an ideology behind it. And the ideology behind it is that they want change but that they want gradual change. They don't want a violent revolution: they want gradual reforms in their country. They're quite diverse.

It was very comfortable. There were dorm beds, about eight in a room, or you could have your own room. They don't provide guided tours. What they generally do is that if they like you, they take you for informal tours. It's in the central city and very handy to many of the places that a visitor would like to see, such as the Saint Nicholas Russian Orthodox Church, the Azadi Tower, the Milad Tower, the Imam Mosque, the Imamzadeh Saleh Mosque, the Imam Jaafar Sadegh Mosque, the Golestan Palace, the Treasury of National Jewels, the US Den of Espionage (formerly known as the US Embassy!), the Tabiat Bridge, the Sa'dabad Historical Complex of former palaces-turned-museums in the hills above Tehran, the Ali Akbar Holy Shrine, and others!

The Imam Mosque, formerly the Shah Mosque

99

The Imam Mosque

The Imamzadeh Saleh Mosque, as blue as the Imam Mosque is pink

The author on the steps of the Imamzadeh Saleh Mosque

Lads hanging around outside

One of the things I noticed first in Tehran was way that the interiors of palaces and mosques often seemed to be decorated with lots of tiny fragments of mirrors. Several people have said that it's like being "inside a diamond."

Mirror Hall of the Green Palace, in the Sa'dabad Complex

Bedroom in the Green Palace of the Sa'dabad Complex

The custom arose in the 1500s, when glass mirrors not too different from the kind we have in our bathrooms and bedrooms, today, were just starting to be manufactured in Europe.

For thousands of years before that date, the most common kind of mirror had been a polished sheet of bronze; the dark metal they make statues out of.

The poor quality of such a reflection is said to lie behind the biblical expression "through a glass, darkly," a metaphor for limited understanding. Many believe that the original, ancient text refers to an image in a bronze mirror. In the 1600s, when the influential King James translation of the Bible came out, a mirror was widely known in English as a 'glass'. For, by that time the glassblowers of Venice had perfected a way of bonding a thin layer of a silvery metal, which made a better mirror than bronze but was very prone to tarnishing, to a protective sheet of glass. The metal remained bright on the side that could be seen by looking through the glass. The result was called a looking-glass, or glass for short.

The image seen through such a glass wasn't dark at all. Still, the translators had to put something down!

The new, Venetian mirrors were a hit even in distant Persia. Unfortunately, many of them didn't survive the trip by sailing-ship and camel. To avoid wasting the smashed bits, Persian craft workers came up with the idea of making them into mirror tiles and arranging them so that they reflected into each other, like the facets of a diamond.

Here are a couple of pictures of the women's prayer room inside the Imamzadeh Saleh Mosque that also show the technique. I was to come across it again and again in Iran.

Getting back to the See You in Iran Hostel, it is run by a loose group of 30 to 100 people. A lot of them have wealthy relatives in the UK and the USA; their relatives have a commitment to Iran as they still see themselves as Persians. I had a huge number of conversations. Sometimes I would go down and somebody on the desk would say "put your hijab on!" and I wouldn't. I just point-blank refused to wear it in the lounge, and I refused to wear it anywhere inside the hostel generally.

You don't have to wear Islamic head-coverings in private household space. Of course, whether somewhere like a lounge qualified as that was a bit of a grey area.

I didn't openly argue, as obviously I didn't want to have an argument about wearing the hijab. I just didn't wear it. One guy at the counter said that the lounge area and kitchen definitely was a public space. But forget it, I didn't want to wear it. And that was it. And others never said boo. Most of the girls working there did wear their hijab, though.

It is widely acceptable to have the hijab on just half your scalp. A lot of Iranian women wear a lot of lipstick, makeup and nail polish. They manage to look very glamorous, in ways that make me think of old photos of movie stars.

We forget that, not so long ago, any respectable person setting foot outside their front door in the West was expected to have their head covered. For the women the dress code was something along the lines of hat, gloves and pearls — or a headscarf — and gentlemen wore hats, too, at least if they were proper gentlemen.

Come to think of it, it wasn't unknown for Western women to wear veils as well! Although that usually meant that somebody had died.

Of course, nobody in the West went so far as to put a bag over their head with a little slit for the eyes. But then again, until recently, Middle Eastern Muslims hardly ever dressed like that either, unless they were nomads with a practical interest in not having their faces sandpapered off by desert winds.

Grace Kelly and Frank Sinatra on the set of 'High Society', 1956.
Photo via Wikimedia Commons, which claims no evidence of US copyright renewal.

So, up to a point, you could say that the Iranian headscarf custom is merely a bit old-fashioned; kind of like going back to the 1950s. I found that some Iranians wanted gradual change, perhaps along the lines of not having the headscarf custom actually *enforced* by the IRGC and other busybodies. And others were happy with things the way they were.

So, they were a diverse group in the See You in Iran Hostel. But what they were most concerned about was promoting a positive image of Iran to the Western World. And it definitely was safe for women to travel.

There were many places where I could eat. Central Tehran had some amazing cafes. I could get taxis straight away. I also used Snapp, a local equivalent of Uber. And it was at the See You in Iran Hostel that I discovered the Mah Card, which they sell.

The best thing about Iran was that they do treat foreigners with a certain degree of respect. I was never challenged in a lot of the restaurants where I ate, when I took my hijab off, they were just too polite.

It's quite common for Iranian women not to wear their hijabs when not actually on the street. As I've mentioned, they aren't required to wear them in private, which would be ridiculous, but only in public. Still, what does "in public" mean? In the street where they might be seen by the morality police, yes. But people push the boundaries in semi-private, semi-public spaces like restaurants.

I was amazed to discover that you could get a gondola up to a ski-field from Tehran. The lofty Alborz mountains are very close, and there are lots of places where you can get up into the hills that overlook the city, to get away from the 'hot place'.

I had been planning to strike out on my own after Tehran. But for the rest of my journey, I decided to take a package route. I was basically tired. I'd been travelling for eight months and just didn't have the energy to individually negotiate buses, taxis, trains and planes.

I had a friend who owns a tourist hotel in Nepal. Because Iran's so mountainous, a lot of Iranians are into climbing. Iranian climbers often travel abroad: to Nepal and to Europe. So, my Nepalese hotelier friend put me on to some young Iranian guides; and I decided that I would do a guided tour of Iran because I was feeling a little bit tired.

My Nepalese friend recommended a guide named Azad, who was a member of the Iranian Mountain Club. There was also a woman he worked with, named Kimi. I decided to negotiate a tour with both of them, a tour which would cost US $100 a day including accommodation and meals, from the 8th to the 19th of October. I thought this was definitely reasonable.

While I was in Tehran, Azad took me up the mountain. We did yoga, because he was a yoga instructor as well.

Also, I engaged their help to see some of the other sights of Tehran.

Azad in a hilltop teahouse

Azad trying out a tent in the hills

Kimi and I at the Tabiat Bridge

After learning to be a mountaineer in Iran, Azad had started working overseas as a tour guide. He took a lot of people over to Europe and Sri Lanka and his family told him not to go back to Iran but to be a refugee. Yet he wanted to live in his own country, so he came back.

Kimi was a qualified mechanical engineer but decided that she was going to run her own restaurant, which had amazing artwork on the walls. She was also doing a radio show and making money from podcasting. So, that was part of their overall strategy for survival.

112

Artwork in Kimi's Café

I spent probably about five days in Tehran, and I did a lot.

I went to some beautiful mosques, including the Imamzadeh Ṣaleh Mosque. I went to the women's prayer area, and I had to put on a full-length black chador before going in.

I really enjoyed visiting the treasury of the jewels of the previous Imperial dynasties in the National Jewelry Museum of Iran, which is probably the most fabulous public collection of jewelry, including transparent cups made entirely out of gold and rubies.

The collection included a globe of the world made out of 34 kg of gold and 51,366 gemstones, with emeralds for the sea and rubies for the land. There were lots of crowns. And the actual Peacock Throne itself.

Much of the jewelry was very well made and in the best of taste, at least if you didn't count ostentatious showpieces like the gold-and-jewels globe. As always, the small pieces were the most charming ones.

What's it all worth? According to the catalogue:

No one knows the answer to this question. . . . the Treasury of National Jewels is on a level that even the most expert evaluators of the world have not been able to calculate the price of this collection.

It was a testament to the skill of the Persian craft-worker, which the museum obviously honoured. All the same, why was a revolutionary regime putting the crown jewels of a deposed emperor on display? The catalogue does have an answer to that question, of sorts:

Before you are overwhelmed by its glitter, consider the historic reasons for the collection these jewels. . . . The Treasury, on the one hand, depicts the culture and civilization of the Iranian people who have had an adventurous past, and on the other hand, repeats the silent tears of oppressed people who worked hard and instead the rulers, could show off their arrogance and power with their gold and jewels.

There were flags hanging that had a lion on them, actually a lion and a sun. Flags that looked like this:

State flag of Iran 1907–1980 in standardised form *by MrInfo2012, CC-BY-SA 4.0 via Wikimedia Commons*

I'd also noticed the lion-and-sun motif on the walls of the Golestan Palace. Here's another look at one of those.

The oldest known Persian lion-and-sun design shows Artaxerxes II, the ruler of Persia around 400 BCE, paying homage to a lion with a woman on top who has the sun radiating behind her.

In those days lots of other state symbols were in use, including an eagle, a four-pointed star, a winged lion, and a lion and a bull in combat. The lion-and-sun didn't become the sole symbol of the Persian state until the Middle Ages. In those days, the lion was held to symbolise the physical power of the state and the sun the Muslim religion watching over the rulers.

All the same, in 1980, the Islamic Republic dropped the lion and sun motif from the national flag in favour of more overtly Islamic imagery based on stylised inscriptions of the name of God and the invocation of God's greatness. The national coat of arms underwent the same changes.

Current Iranian flag in Abbaniyeh mountain village, photo by Nick Taylor, 2008. CC-BY-2.0 via Wikimedia Commons, sharpened slightly.

Like the jewel museum, the Golestan Palace was absolutely amazing and beautiful, and I spent the whole day there. It is the most important and historic royal palace in Tehran. It's vast, and is the surviving part of an even larger complex that was a bit like the Forbidden City in Beijing. It contains many rooms in incredible styles, including two lined with reflecting fragments of mirror glass in the style I've already explained above, whereby craftsmen making a virtue out of necessity, with bits of broken mirror, evolved a complete new art form.

The very first glitter ball? Golestan Palace

Stained glass window in the Edifice of the Sun, at the Golestan Palace

The Reception (Throne) Hall

Portico outside the Reception Hall

Part of the exterior, Golestan Palace

The Karim Khani Nook; note the translucency of the marble!

121

The Marble Throne

Behind the Marble Throne

Room in the Building of the Windcatchers

Golestan Palace also has humbler parts, still quite elegant in their own way; this corridor was probably used by the servants, I imagine.

The Golestan Palace was mostly built by the Qajar Dynasty, the one that first established Tehran as the nation's capital in 1796.

Videos actually give you the best idea of what it's like to roam around inside, and I made sure I got a few:

It even includes psychedelically-decorated warehouses for the royal travelling-tents!

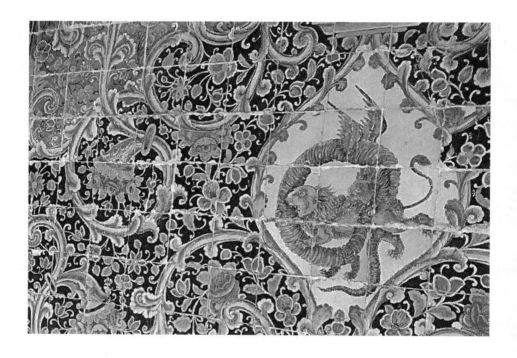

It's enough to make you go dizzy! Anyway, you can see where the hippies got the idea from.

These palace complexes are now mostly museums, of course, displaying royal collections to the public. At Golestan, the Qajars collected the colourful native costumes of their various nationalities and tribes that they ruled. This must be a gold-mine for modern-day researchers, or for anyone wanting to design authentic costumes for a movie set in the old times.

The other important palace-museum complex in Tehran is Sa'dabad, up in the hills and more of a summer palace, apparently. We went up there on a wet day, which seemed appropriate. Here are some photos taken at Sa'dabad. The first one is of a statue of Arash the Archer, an important national figure in Iran, a bit like William Tell.

Like Golestan, Sa'dabad was also mostly built under the Qajars.

Here are some photos of the complex, including a public map. It's pretty vast given that it's supposed to be a modest woodland retreat. It's true that none of the individual buildings are anything like as big as what's at Golestan.

One of the Shah's modest chalets at Sa'dabad

131

Another tasteful structure

A Chinese dog

Scenes from Persian mythology

The office of the Shah

The last-ever Persian tiger?

With some women at Sa'dabad for a celebration

As I say, places like Sa'dabad are basically museums, now. There's an art gallery, with works done in the Qajar period and more modern art as well. Some of the Qajar art was done in Western styles such as this painting, called 'The Priests'.

135

And here are some more modern works, all by Iranian artists as well I believe.

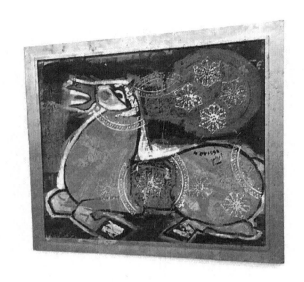

For instance, while I saw some modern art at Sa'dabad, I was to see a lot more at a dedicated modern art museum downtown, the Tehran Museum of Contemporary Art, which had been instigated by the Shah's third and final wife, Empress Farah, and opened by her in 1977, two years before the revolution. Fortunately, it is still open, with many works by contemporary Iranian artists.

Iranian women admire Farah for the active part she played in promoting the arts and the status of women in general.

Incidentally, the Iranian film industry is a world-leader, both in terms of films made in Iran and films made by exiles, like *Persepolis,* a dramatised account of the revolution in cartoon form. Again, it's that artistic tradition that's so strong in Iran, and seems to keep bursting out in new ways, I suppose.

Before, I mentioned how the American Embassy in Tehran was occupied, soon after the revolution, by students who had demanded that the Americans send back the Shah. This episode is known as the Iran Hostage Crisis. The Shah was in America, in the hope of some kind of last-ditch treatment for his cancer, when the embassy was occupied.

Bearing in mind that the Shah and his empress had both been sentenced to death by the Islamic regime, there was no way that the Americans were going to send the Shah back. They were no doubt a bit relieved when the treatment didn't work and he expired halfway through 1980; though it was still some months before the Iranians let the hostages go.

Some students who led the US Embassy occupation

The former American Embassy — the two countries still haven't restored normal relations — is now decorated with anti-American posters and graffiti, and has been tuned into a museum documenting American espionage and subversion. Some of it's true; the occupiers got their hands on all kinds of incredibly secret stuff. In the months that the embassy was occupied, they were even able to put together documents that the Americans had shredded. Perhaps that was another reason for storming the embassy.

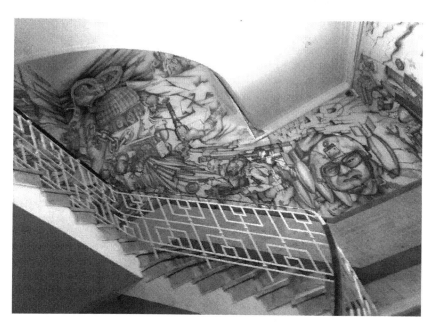

Even here, we see the influence of the fine old Persian decorative tradition. I could imagine that if the Americans ever re-opened the embassy, they might want to keep one or two of the murals:

Some of it's a bit uglier, of course. I had a photo taken in front of the most notorious piece of artwork, one that's often used in media stories about Iran-vs-USA tension.

I saw one or two Iranian women with the hijab off at the Golestan Palace; they also had a 'White Wednesday' protest against the compulsory-head-covering laws. I decided that if I saw one Iranian woman with no hijab, off mine came: you know, solidarity sister, just take it off.

Some German women were wearing scarves and one of them turned to me and said I was being disrespectful. And I said I wasn't being disrespectful, I just did what young Iranian women wanted to do!

And I also managed to find a massage in Iran. I looked on TripAdvisor. Women were working in the sauna. That was quite common.

At the hostel, I heard that a lot of people were really worried about the disappearance of the middle class in Iran. Everyone was worried about the future with the US embargo. Sanction were being progressively tightened, in ways that gave American firms and other overseas firms that trade with America time to wind down their activities. Stage One had happened and Stage Two was coming in in a month's time, on 4 November.

Things like American-made aviation parts, the lack of which was supposed to have made Iran's domestic flights unsafe, would once more be restricted after having been available for a while. About twenty countries had stopped buying oil from Iran. The Americans said that they would allow China, India, Greece, Taiwan, Italy, Japan, South Korea and Turkey to go on buying oil from Iran until 2 May 2019, but then they had to stop or face sanctions of their own from the USA (China has since defied this pronouncement.)

Among the young people I met, none of them wanted children. They didn't want to bring children into this world and didn't have confidence in the future of Iran, which I thought was extremely sad. I didn't quite realise why this was at the time, and it was only when I saw the dried-up river in Isfahan, and found out about Lake Urmia and the country's population issues, that the penny dropped completely.

I've heard of people not wanting to have kids for fear they would have to grow up in a global warming apocalypse. Well, in

Iran, such an eco-apocalypse is already in full swing. The country's some decades ahead of the rest of us in that respect. It's as though it's 2050 already in Iran, environmentally speaking.

Most of these people didn't believe in traditional Islam at all, either. I think the revolution has discredited the religion, by shoving it down everyone's throats.

Well, what more can I say about Tehran? A lot of people use motorbikes, for one thing. And it was very safe to walk around by day and by night.

A lot of the people in Iran also spend time in the plazas and squares. This was something I noticed in Tehran, and everywhere else I went in Iran.

Street life in Shiraz

It's an old fashioned outdoor civic culture, still largely untouched by the kind of privatised suburban existence we often have in the West, or by huge amounts of car-traffic either for that matter. Some Iranian boulevards seem to have more footpath than carriageway for cars, the two separated by planter boxes and solid-looking blocks.

Like so much else that's of a leisurely and civilised nature, the Persians probably invented the pavement cafe as well

I mean seriously, for coffee didn't catch on in Europe till long after it had become popular in the Middle East.

I didn't see many whole families out on the street, though.

There had been a move to allow foreign women not to wear the hijab, but this never got through.

CHAPTER 11

The Culture of Food

ALONG with strong artistic traditions and a civilised street life, the Iranians also have amazing food! It's 'Middle Eastern' of course, with lots of emphasis on flat breads and sauces, rice, yoghurt and hummus, dates, lemons, kebabs, sqoooshy eggplant dishes, salad greens, and all sorts of other wholesome ingredients that people buy in the bazaars.

Kimi (right) and myself in a traditional-food restaurant

Is there anything that's distinctive about Persian food, as opposed to Middle Eastern food in general? Well, to be honest I don't know enough to say whether there's anything that people cook up in Iran that's *never* thought of as a local dish in some other Middle Eastern country, too.

But anyhow, I can think of some things that are associated with Iran in general. One is the use of a lot of tomato paste in stews. For instance, as with this stew of meat and beans or chickpeas, which comes with a great many variations, called dizi. The name dizi actually refers to the little ramekins that it traditionally comes in, which probably help to keep it warm.

160

Dizi, served in the Darband district of Tehran. *Photograph by Vahid Sarabi (2017), Tasnim News Agency, CC-BY-SA 4.0 via Wikimedia Commons.*

There's also a thick soup called ash, or āsh strictly speaking, which Iranians distinguish from soup (sup). I think Kimi has just been served some āsh in this photo.

Another classic Persian dish is polow, also known around the world as pilau, pilaff, plov or any one of a multitude of variations, made from things like bits of meat, nuts, raisins and vegetables mixed in with rice, which has often been cooked in stock. One of the reasons that there are so many different names for the dish is that just about every district in the Middle East and the Caucasus has its own regional version, or versions. But it's generally thought of as a Persian dish all the same.

Polow. *Photo by Tamorlan (2012), CC-BY-SA 3.0, via Wikimedia Commons.*

In Iranian cooking, it's also common to use pungent herbs and spices like dill and cilantro (fresh coriander leaves), garlic, turmeric and savory to give a bit of something extra even to quite mundane meal bases, such as broad beans. To drink, you might want pomegranate juice, or a salty yoghurt drink called doogh. A sauce called delal is made from cilantro, basil and parley ground up with salt for preservation.

There's even Iranian pizza!

Makhloot (mixed) Iranian Pizza. Photo by Namita76 (2018), CC-BY-SA 4.0 via Wikimedia Commons.

And there are a few quite distinctive Iranian desserts as well, such as saffron-flavoured ice cream and a dessert called falude, originally invented in Shiraz, which is a mixture of vermicelli (seriously) in a half-frozen mixture of syrup and rose water.

Each district of Iran also has distinctive regional variations. Basically, there's no end to Iranian cuisine, an important part of the country's glory just like the rest of its culture.

CHAPTER 12

Isfahan: No water, Revolutionary Guards as neighbours, but much art

An aerial image of downtown Isfahan. *Imagery ©2019 Maxar Technologies, map data ©2019 Google.*

FOUR hundred kilometres south of Tehran, halfway to the Persian Gulf, Isfahan is another famous city. Itself a former capital of Persia, Isfahan — which the locals pronounce *Esfahan* — is famous for its architecture, and also for being an early example of town planning.

Isfahan sits on the river Zayandeh, the biggest river in central Iran. Its name means 'life giver', in the sense that without the Zayandeh, the region would be a desert.

The river is spanned by several famous bridges, the oldest of which, the Shahrestan Bridge, has foundations dating back almost to classical antiquity. Its shape is scientifically bowed upriver in the middle, so that the force of floods will be more effectively resisted. Which is, presumably, why it's still there.

Other famous, historical bridges of Isfahan include the Marnan Bridge, the Si-o-se-pol, the Khaju Bridge, and the Joubi Bridge. Both the Khaju Bridge and the Si-o-se-pol (which means bridge of thirty-three arches) are on two levels, with covered space underneath and with alcoves and pavilions. They are popular meeting-places for the people of the city, a city which they pretty much symbolise. These two bridges also have weirs, intended to regulate and broaden the river in the downtown area and make sure that there is always plenty of standing water, to cool and refresh the parklands alongside.

The Si-o-se-pol

167

The Weir of the Si-o-se-pol

There are also more modern bridges, of course.

The Ferdowsi bridge, named after Ferdowsi, one of the first great Persian poets of the Middle Ages

One thing you might have noticed is that whether the bridges are old or new, you didn't need them to get across the river when I took these photos. You could even stand in the middle of the river for a better shot!

The Khaju Bridge and its Weir

Pavilion on the Khaju Bridge

As I mentioned up front, Iran is suffering from a huge water crisis at present, caused by a variety of factors ranging from climate change to the effect of international sanctions. The Zayandeh river is flowing again, but when I was there, it was enduring an eighteen-month dry spell. These dry spells apparently started happening about ten years ago. They really get on the nerves of the people of Isfahan, who are apparently much more cheerful when the 'life giver' is flowing, than when it is not.

Isfahan is a planned city, perhaps the original 'garden city', developed by the Safavid Dynasty of Persian rulers (1501–1736) as their capital, just as Tehran was developed by the Qajars. The bridges, with their weirs intended to trap standing water, were a part of the Safavid planning scheme, which also included a huge belt of greenery around the city, kept green by canals fed from the Zayandeh (though it's not so green at the moment)

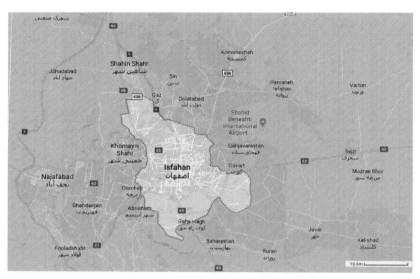

Isfahan, with its Green Belt. Map data ©2019 Google.

A dried-up canal in the green belt

Within the city, one of the most famous avenues in the world, Chaharbagh Boulevard, which dates back all the way to 1596, runs through the middle of the city, in a straight line, for six kilometres. The name of the boulevard means 'four gardens'. This is a reference to the four gardens of Paradise mentioned in the Koran and to a common design of parks in Muslim countries, whereby a park is divided into four quadrants in order to honour the same idea here on Earth.

A very modern-looking Chaharbagh Boulevard in 1705, by Cornelis de Bruyn. Via Wikimedia Commons.

The great, tree-lined boulevard is still there, of course, with lots of parks along it. In general, Iranian cities are great for walking around in. Here are some photos that I took in the area, either on

173

Chaharbagh Boulevard itself or its side streets, which are impressive too.

The Safavids also created a huge public square, the Naqsh-e Jahan Square, also known as the Shah Square or, these days, the Imam Square. Safavid Isfahan became an important 'world city', well-known to Europeans, who published engravings of its wondrous sights.

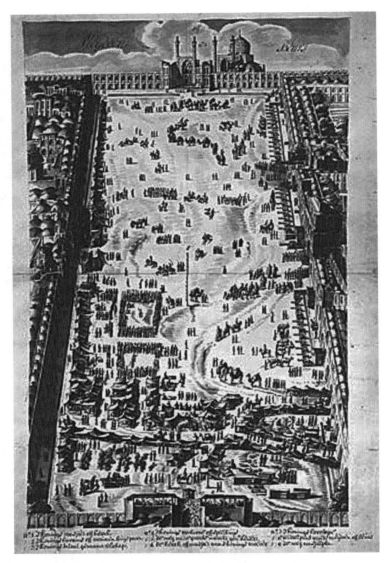

Naqsh-e Jahan Square in 1703, styled as the 'Great Bazaar of Isfahan', by G. Hofsted van Essen. Public domain work via Wikimedia Commons.

Naqsh-e Jahan Square as I saw it

The total population of Isfahan today is about two million, much less than Tehran, but it is still a big city.

Azad and I went to Isfahan from Tehran by bus. It was quite an enjoyable journey, even though it was a long ride. Iranian inter-city coaches are quite luxurious (and cheap as well).

At one of the bus stops, I remember, Azad helpfully ordered my food. It was rice and beans. And then he very nicely helped some other women who couldn't speak any Persian.

He helped them to order their meal too. And then one of them, who was from Spain, came over and said that they didn't talk to men.

178

I asked her why. She said that she had been hassled by men beyond belief and she said that she had come to Iran to get to know the women of Iran, and that the men would get in the way. And that all the women she had gone with had been hassled.

And she looked at me and kind of hinted that the men wouldn't hassle me, whatever that meant precisely.

I think some Westerners have the idea that women in Iran are more oppressed than they really are, and that they have to be saved from these terrible Middle Eastern men. In reality, I was finding the country to be intensely civilised. The women I went with had no problems from the menfolk of Iran.

Following our encounter with the sisterhood, we arrived in Isfahan, where we were to stay with a friend of Azad's. This man was trying to save a local mountain. It had a gondola going up half of it and he didn't want a gondola going up the rest of it.

The mountain Azad's friend was trying to save

179

So, I asked him: what was it like to protest in Iran? And he said that it was easier than what outsiders thought, that you could make your concerns heard but that you couldn't just openly protest.

That if you openly protested you would be reprimanded. You could go into an office and lodge a complaint. He said that two years before, in Isfahan, women had had acid thrown in their faces because people felt Isfahan had become too liberal and that women were showing too much of their hair and wearing too much make up.

He was very scared and said to me that I should cover my head a lot more, and he even insisted that the shirt that I was wearing (because I was wearing a short blue shirt with long sleeves that came just down past my waist, with a long pink and white dress that covered all of my body) was a problem. He said that Isfahan was very conservative.

It was great to stay with a local, but he was very nervous about having me stay because his neighbours were conservative IRGC types and some flew the IRGC flag.

We went out for dinner. I had my own room on the 3rd floor and we would leave early in the morning.

After that, I got a room in a place called the Caravanserai, an amazing old-school hotel that only cost US $40 a night.

And we spent our evenings in bazaars and dining out on the usual, amazing, Iranian food.

Still, Azad's friend was more than hospitable. We would go around to his place for breakfast.

Azad took me to a district called Vank on the south side of the river, and to Vank's Christian, Armenian cathedral. Earlier Shahs had encouraged Armenians to settle in this area during the 1500s and 1600s. They had formed a recognised, officially protected community of artisans.

The entrance to the Vank Cathedral's enclosed courtyard. The cathedral itself has a big Persian-style dome on top.

Frescoes in Vank Cathedral

Armenian illustrated manuscript—the Bible?

Check out the monster devouring the sinners, at bottom right!

Azad had a cousin who had done a PhD on Kurdish participation in the Ottoman Empire's genocide of the Armenians (which I've mentioned in my blog posts on Mount Ararat). The Ottoman Empire had invaded Iran during World War One, as I mentioned, so that even in some parts of Iran the Armenians hadn't been safe. Across the courtyard from the Vank Cathedral there is a museum that combined more cheerful exhibits with material on the genocide of the Armenians. I was humbled to have seen that.

Traditional costume of Armenian girls in the Isfahan region

The twin peaks of Mount Ararat, the national mountain of Armenia, located roughly at the point where modern-day Armenia, Turkey and Iran all join together. Mount Ararat is just inside the Turkish border, today.

Some of the major sites of genocide

The Armenians used to inhabit much of Eastern Turkey, from the Caspian Sea and the Black Sea to the Mediterranean. The lands of the Armenians also extended into the old Russian Empire and the later Soviet Union. As with Azerbaijan, it was the Soviet part of historical Armenia that became an independent country in 1991.

After the Vank Cathedral and its disturbing museum, we did a tour of the Ali Qapu palace and the Sheikh Lotf Allah and Imam mosques, which were wrapped around the Naqsh-e Jahan Square. The following photos show details of both mosques.

190

Dome of the Sheikh Lotf Allah Mosque. This was the private chapel of the Safavid Shahs. The Imam mosque was public.

Entrance to the Imam Mosque

It's interesting to note that while the mosques are an aethereal blue, the palace is hot pink!

Portico of the Ali Qapu Palace

Fresco of a Persian woman in the palace portico, just visible in the previous photo

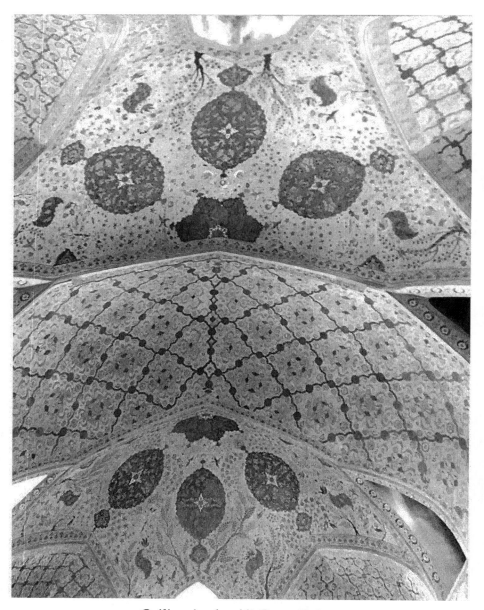

Ceiling in the Ali Qapu Palace

Like the royal tent warehouses at Golestan, It's all a bit head-spinning once more. It was time to get some coffee . . . Except the coffee-house looked like a pink palace itself, smashed-mirror ceiling and all!

Finally, we found somewhere a bit more proletarian.

Ready for more dazzling sights, we went to Hasht Behesht, a mini-palace on Chaharbagh Boulevard.

The most exquisite tilework in all of Iran is said to be found in two places in downtown Isfahan: firstly, at the Sheikh Lotf Allah Mosque, one of the two mosques on Naqsh-e Jahan Square, and secondly at the Chahar Bagh Theological School, right next to the gardens of Hasht Behesht.

Sheikh Lotf Allah mosque was the private chapel of the Safavid Shahs and was only opened to the public later on.

You can click here for a 360-degree panorama of Chahar Bagh Boulevard and the entrance to the theological school, from 360cities. This also gives you a good idea of what the boulevard is like.

I took some photos inside the theological school, which is open to the public. Just as Ali Qapu is pink and the mosques of Naqsh-e Jahan are blue, the Chahar Bagh Theological School seems to be mainly decorated in yellow.

I'm not sure what this building was, but it's pretty interesting as well. Note the animals!

The next day we toured the bridges of Isfahan, well into the evening. These are not just bridges, but also centres of the city's social life.

At night people sing at the bridges. They celebrate, light campfires, and take pictures. The bridges were designed to take in the sun above the waters, and all kinds of poetical stuff was intended to take place. So, it was really sad that they were all without water when I was there. People were wondering if they would ever get their river back.

But on a happier note, the architecture of Isfahan was absolutely stunning: the most amazing I have ever seen.

We went to the music museum. And that was amazing. It's got the music from all parts of Iran.

On the last day my host went to pour water and there was no water coming out of the tap. Lack of water was an issue in the region. The reason the river stopped, he said, was because the farmers were using the water, so the cities didn't get any water. It was made worse by corruption, he said; apparently, Isfahan didn't have enough political pull to keep getting water.

We walked along the riverbank. And it was really weird just walking along a riverbank by a dried-up river. At the Ferdowsi Bridge I saw some artwork of birds erected in honour of Ferdowsi, which people now said had taken on a second significance: the flight of birdlife from the dry river and the withering green belt.

And all the photos on TripAdvisor show Isfahan with a flowing river. For a city so famous for its greenery and bridges, it really is a disaster!

So, there is some protest, but the authoritarian nature of the Islamic Republic, which is paranoid about being overthrown just like the Shah before, prevents protest from being too overt. There have been massive political protests against the Islamic regime in the comparatively recent past; but they were cracked down on severely.

The suppression of large-scale protest probably means that all kinds of corruption and mismanagement of things like mountains and water can just go on without much fear of people taking to the streets over it; even though issues of this nature have nothing to do with whether people are trying to overturn the wider Islamic regime or not.

But there was one good thing we also did on the last day I was there, and that was to visit yet another palace, Chehel Sotoun. Chehel Sotoun means 'forty columns', and it refers to the reflection of the twenty actual columns of the palace in a reflecting pool in the centre of some magnificent gardens.

I thought I'd seen it all when it came to interiors, but Chehel Sotoun was really something else again. I liked the shiny, metallic effect. And just like the costumes at Golestan, the Safavid murals at Chehel Sotoun are very valuable for researchers who want to know how people dressed, and danced, in those days.

It's bookended by another structure, at the far end of the reflecting pool.

And on the last day we also saw this attractive little prayer-nook, with flags.

Oh yes, one final thing. In one of the shops where I was buying souvenirs, I saw one of those flags that had a lion and sun on it, like the ones in the Treasury of the National Jewels. For about three days, nobody told me what purpose it served. Then I found out that it was the old flag of Iran under the last Shah. I wanted to buy it, but it turned out that it wasn't for sale.

CHAPTER 13

Shiraz: Poets and an ancient culture

I spent two or three nights in Shiraz. It was the home of prophets and poets. And by tradition the people were really laid back, known for having siestas.

Yet I also spoke to people who were very worried about the American and international sanctions. It was health care that they were mostly worried about, health care and access to drugs for severe diseases. Women couldn't even get sanitary products, and sick people couldn't get necessary drugs.

As with aircraft parts, there were supposed to be exemptions for medicines essential to life and safety. In reality the supplies of all these things were drying up all the same, and the problems were being made worse by general economic hardship.

Shop owners were worried too, as there weren't any tourists thanks to sanctions and tensions with the West.

I stayed in a beautiful place surrounded by a garden in the inner city. Azad got his privacy at night in the hotel.

Inner city gardens

A lot of Iranians come back for the summer from overseas and stay in relatives' houses. I had a conversation with one of these expatriates where I was staying.

We met a friend of Kimi's who couldn't get out of the country. She applied for a work visa in Canada and a student visa. She was trying to get out, though her husband had a good job in Iran.

I was doing my bit to prop up the local economy, buying a clock and food platters in Isfahan, and wall hangings here in Shiraz.

We'd done a lot in Isfahan, so we needed to slow down. My photos of Shiraz are just of beautiful things: scenes of the city at night, mosques, tombs of poets. There was no shortage of delightful subjects, from the Shiraz Citadel and glowing mosques, to parks and cafes.

The Shiraz Citadel

Here are some photos of what's probably the most famous thing in Shiraz, the Nasir-ol-Molk Mosque, a great tourist attraction because of the light cast by its stained-glass windows in the morning.

Elsewhere, Shiraz also seems to have a decorative style of its own, a sort of gothic, wood-carving style that looks like it wouldn't be out of place in a European cathedral. You can spot it in these photos.

And of course, we visited the tombs of the poets Hafez and Sa'adi. Here is the tomb of Sa'adi, the author of *Golestan*, which has no doubt got more and more grand over the years.

It seems as though I'm thinking it's a bit over the top! The tomb of Hafez is more modest.

That's all, folks. There's a big garden pavilion that you go through to get to Hafez's tomb. But that still somehow seems to make more sense than building a house for someone who's not in a position to enjoy it.

CHAPTER 14

Naqsh-e Rostam, Persepolis and Pasgardae

W E did one strenuous thing, though, while we were in Shiraz. And that was to head out of town to the ancient monuments of Naqsh-e Rostam, Perspolis and Pasgardae.

About sixty kilometres out of Shiraz, on the left side of highway 65 as you head north out of town, Naqsh-e Rostam is an ancient necropolis, or city of the dead, in which tombs of ancient Persian emperors have been hewn into the side of a rocky hill.

The hill also bears carvings celebrating the victories of ancient Persia, especially the several times the Romans got their butts kicked by the Persians, to the point of having to pay tribute of 500,000 gold pieces to the Persian emperor and even having their own emperor taken prisoner.

This sort of thing didn't happen too often in the ancient world, where it was usually the Romans dishing out the punishment to some Celtic tribe or other. And so, it was deemed worthy of commemoration.

Here are the actual tombs of really famous early Persian emperors such as Darius the Great, who fought the Greeks at the Battle of Marathon, and, so it's thought, also, of Xerxes the Great, the one who fought the 300 Spartans at Thermopylae. It's remarkable that everyone in the West knows about the Greeks,

Romans and Egyptians but not about the equivalent monuments and tombs of the Persians.

Royal tombs at Naqsh-e Rostam

The Persian emperor Shahpur I taking Roman Emperor Valerian (standing) prisoner in 260CE while an earlier Roman Emperor, Philip the Arab, kneels in supplication. In 244 CE Philip the Arab ceded Armenia to the Persians and agreed to pay 500,000 gold coins to Persia as tribute. Valerian decided to do something about Rome's shock relegation to the second division under Philip (who didn't last too long in the top job), only to suffer a worse humiliation. This carving is at the necropolis of Naqsh-e Rostam, just outside Shiraz.

On the next page, I've got a photo of a carving of Ardashir the Unifier, founder of the Sassanian dynasty (the one under which Persia proved to be more than a match for the Romans) and, as such, another important Persian emperor. Ardashir receives the blessing of the Zoroastrian God of the universe, light, and wisdom, Ahura Mazda.

(Both Mazda light bulbs and the Mazda brand of automobiles and trucks were named after Ahura Mazda. Whether that's a compliment or not, you'd have to ask the Zoroastrians.)

This is another interesting structure at Naqsh-e Rostam, the so-called Ka'ba of Zoroaster, which stands in front of the tomb of Darius II, who lived in the time of the ancient Greeks.

The name was bestowed by Muslims many centuries ago, on the grounds that it resembled the Ka'ba at Mecca; they supposed that it must have been a similarly sacred site to the ancient Zoroastrians. It's now known that Persians of the Sassanian dynasty called it the Foundation House. But apart from that, not much else is known about the supposed Ka'ba. It must have been important, but in what way precisely, nobody knows. Or like Darius II, they're not telling.

241

On the other side of the modern highway lies Persepolis, the ancient ceremonial capital of Persia that was burned by the Greeks under Alexander the Great in 330 BCE (I don't think they call him "the Great" in Iran). Persepolis is a Greek name, meaning 'Persian City'.

Persepolis is a name that has stuck to the ancient capital, even though it was bestowed by those who came, marvelled at its magnificence, and then burned the place to the ground.

As to why the Alexandrians burnt the city, this is a bit of a mystery, as Alexander normally sought to win over the people he had just conquered (or 'liberated'). And destroying their most sacred site wasn't a good way to go about capturing the hearts and minds of the Persians.

Some say that Persepolis was burnt in revenge for the Persians having fired the Acropolis some 150 years before. Which seems a long time to hold a grudge.

Another story holds that Alexander's soldiers burned the place down after they got drunk and were foolish enough to listen to a woman who said it it would be really good fun to set fire to the place. Of course, it should be borne in mind that the men of ancient Greece almost ritually blamed their misfortunes on the doings of horrible or foolish women such as the Harpies, the Furies, the Medusa, Medea, and Pandora who opened the box. So, this version is just a bit too mythic and should be taken with a grain of salt, apart from the soldiers-getting-drunk bit. Which probably did happen.

Others say it just was an accident, possibly caused by the soldiers getting drunk and knocking things over. Which probably did happen as well.

A surprisingly large amount of the stonework is still there, including regularly-ordered foundation piles. But the wooden beams and decks are, of course, all gone, with the result that Persepolis looks surprising similar to a building site, awaiting a delivery of timber that will never come.

The Terrace of Persepolis, which was partly natural and partly built-up. It is 18 metres high, for the most part. Most of the complex is on top of the Terrace.

Another view of the Terrace: Ruins of the palace of Artaxerxes I at Persepolis. Photo by Masoud Khalife, CC-BY-SA 4.0 via Wikimedia Commons.

The Lion has long been an emblem of Persia, either alone or in combination with other symbols

The lion of Persia in mythic combat with a bull

'Eagle-Griffon Capital'. A roof beam might have fitted between the two mythical beasts, till the place was burned by the Greeks.

People bearing gifts

Lion Snout

Inscription in Old Persian

Obviously, these photos just scratch the surface of such a huge complex.

Persepolis was vast. They had a downstairs museum that included an amazing history of all the tombs. Persepolis was one of the first UNESCO World Heritage sites, gazetted in 1979.

From Persepolis, we made our way another 70-plus km up the same highway to Pasargadae. This site's main claim to fame is the tomb of Cyrus the Great, the founder of Persia, who died in 530 BCE.

At the time of his death, Cyrus had already amassed an empire stretching from the Balkans to India. The Greek conqueror Alexander the Great, who briefly lorded over the same dominion two hundred years later, visited this very tomb and paid homage to the man who inspired him. Lots of people have done so since, including the Shah in the year 1971, the 2,500th anniversary of the founding of Persia by Cyrus.

Tomb of Cyrus the Great, 2,500-year anniversary of the Persian Empire, 1971. The man in uniform in front of the flag-bearer is probably the Shah. Public domain image via Wikimedia Commons.

This is what the tomb looks like today. It hasn't changed much, save in colour, which changes constantly with the light.

Though it didn't work for the Shah, let's hope that some of Cyrus's magical mojo will rub off on me!

There is no inscription saying that it is Cyrus's tomb. But apparently there was one in the past. And this was the tomb that Alexander visited in the belief that it was Cyrus's, only two hundred years after the founder of Persia had lived. So, we can be reasonably sure.

The now-lost inscription was also the one that is supposed to have invited the visitor from the future not to begrudge Cyrus, once so mighty, the little patch of earth he now occupied.

We visited three other tombs at Pasargadae as well.

Azad and I hired a driver for the day, and we all had lunch at a pizza place. I don't think they had pizza in Cyrus's day! Or then again, maybe they did . . .

And so, I really enjoyed all of that. It was really a packed tour and worthwhile. And then I met up with Kimi, to catch the train to Yazd and the nearby town of Taft, in order to take in quite a different culture.

CHAPTER 15

Yazd and Taft: Towers to catch the wind, and towers of silence

KIMI met me at the Yazd railway station, and we spend the night on a desert safari outside the city. There was a fire burning and we camped for the night under the stars. This wasn't metropolitan Iran anymore. We were now in camel country.

A camel!

The many colours of the desert

Lighting a fire in the desert

After camping out, we arrived at the desert city of Yazd, an old and fabled manufacturing centre on the Silk Road, described by Marco Polo:

It is a good and noble city, and has a great amount of trade. They weave there quantities of a certain silk tissue known as Yasdi, which merchants carry into many quarters to dispose of.

Many other crafts have been carried out in Yazd for just as long. And today, the city has more modern industries as well, such as a fibre optic manufacturing plant.

We stayed in a really beautiful hotel, in a craft area where people painted, made things out of wood, leather, and did Iranian painting and art.

The area was dominated by a public space called Zaiee Square, next to the 11th-century Tomb of the Twelve Imams, a somewhat misleading name as no Imams are buried there. There is a coffee shop next to the 'tomb', which has an interesting eight-sided base to its dome.

The Tomb of the Twelve Imams is done in a style that wouldn't have been the least bit out of place in early Christendom. The sacred architecture only gradually diverged, with Western Christians going in for gothic, and Muslims coming to adopt later Persian styles of mosque-building. In Shiraz, as we've seen, there's also a Muslim version of gothic.

The Tomb of the Twelve Imams

Also next to Zaiee Square is a 15th-century structure known as Alexander's Prison, after a poem by Hafez of Shiraz in which Hafez claimed, or pretended, that the Greek conqueror Alexander had held people prisoner in a deep well there. The well still exists, but the larger structure obviously wasn't there in Alexander's time.

These days, the whole area is a craft-shop district.

There are many towns and cities in the desert areas of Iran, though most are small. They survive because the deserts of Iran contain mountain ranges that capture moisture from the air and create streams that run down to their bases; just like the Alborz, though they don't catch as much.

Yazd is the biggest of Iran's desert towns and cities, with a bit over half a million inhabitants. It's said to be one of the oldest cities in the world, about five thousand years old.

The old town of Yazd is also the largest city made out of mud bricks, or adobe, in the world.

Adobe structures in Yazd

It's the sort of city that the Babylonians might have lived in, except that it's in the modern age.

257

There is also a nearby township called Taft, which is is famous for being an even more authentically Mediaeval town.

What's especially distinctive about the old towns of this area is the way that an indigenous air-conditioning technology developed. A technology perhaps inspired by the fact that the mountains catch the wind.

Yazd, and neighbouring small towns like Taft, are studded with tall towers called badgirs or wind-catchers.

Yazd with badgirs

The passing wind creates a suction effect at the top of the tower, drawing air through underground passages called qanats. The qanats are the passages through which cold water from the mountains flows into the city, to be stored in cisterns called ab anbars. Ingenious!

In cold weather, the wind-catcher can also be rigged so as to blow the cold air downwards and cool the qanat further. This technique can even be used to make ice for food storage and extra cooling in summer, later on.

Ice is made inside these by directing cold water into another kind of storage area called a yakhchal, plus freezing air from the wind-catchers on especially cold desert nights. Ice brought back from the local mountains may also be placed inside the yakhchals to get the freezing process going.

Ab anbars and yakhchals are revealed by beehive-like structures above the ground. The walls of these can be up to two metres thick.

Basically, it's all a bit like something out of *Star Wars,* or *Dune.* Or vice versa, since places like Yazd have been around a lot longer than Hollywood, after all.

They have the same sorts of wind towers in the old town of Dubai, which was populated by merchants from Yazd in the past (there have always been foreigners in Dubai, it seems). In Dubai, the towers are called Bastakia towers. I don't know if there's such an elaborate system of underground waterworks in Dubai, however.

In Yazd, these amazing indigenous technologies are celebrated in a Water Museum, based in the former mansion of a rich merchant. The house itself includes a wind tower and passageways called payabs that descend into the underground waterworks.

An industrial-scale complex of wind towers and ab anbars

A payab, leading down to a qanat

Those who dug the qanats and payabs wore a white garment that made them easier to find in the dark, and which also served as a shroud if the roof fell in.

The Water Museum includes a pavilion with its legs set in a water-trough, now dry. This was so that the merchant's family could sit outside without being troubled by ants, lizards and scorpions. Yazd is a desert city, after all!

One of the rooms in the mansion is decorated with portraits of women, many of them in Western attire of the 1890s or thereabouts.

On average, though, Yazd is a conservative city, more pious than Tehran. So, along with amazing adobe architecture and air conditioning systems that don't use a watt of electricity, Yazd is also famous for its religious processions; especially Ashura, the procession held on the tenth day of the Muslim month of Muharram.

This commemorates the martyrdom of Imam Hussein, a grandson of Islam's founder, Muhammad. Hussein led a rebellion against the Caliph Yazid I, the religious-political leader of all Muslims at the time.

Yazid's father, Caliph Muawiya, had proclaimed Yazid his successor: effectively, as king of the Muslims. This was in defiance of an earlier agreement that the Caliph was always to come to power through a broad, general election that was to be as democratic as possible in the circumstances of the time.

The resulting civil war between royalists and democrats, which Hussein lost along with his head, is an event of colossal significance in Muslim history: and especially significant for Shi'a. In fact the origins of the Sunni-Shi'a split date back to this incident, though Hussein is revered in the Sunni world as well.

Traditionally, the whole episode has been seen in *Braveheart* terms, with Yazid as the evil king: evil in part because he wasn't supposed to be a king in the first place but rather a candidate for presidential office.

The Ayatollahs who led the Islamic Revolution of 1979 represented themselves as successors to Hussein, and the Shah as the evil king.

Religious-political poster of the two supreme leaders

Among Shi'ites, the ceremonies of Ashura include the transportation of a device called a nakhl, a kind of symbolic coffin or hearse, on the shoulders of mourners. The procession is called Nakhl Gardani, that is, the Transportation of the Nakhl.

As with fireworks displays on Guy Fawkes night, there are many nakhls, great and small, depending on people's means. On the next page, there's a picture of me beside a small nakhl at the Amir Chaghmagh mosque complex, which wraps around Yazd's most important town square in a similar fashion to Naqsh-e Jahan in Isfahan, though it isn't as big.

A nakhl. The wooden frame would normally be draped and decorated when the nakhl is carried in a procession.

Nowhere does the custom of the nakhl seem to be more highly developed or widely practiced than in Yazd, a city described by Jalal Al-e-Ahmad, a mid-twentieth century Iranian intellectual, as "Iran's museum of mourning tools." The largest nakhl in all of Iran and possibly the whole of the Shi'ite world stands outside the Amir Chaghmagh mosque.

The Amir Chaghmagh Mosque, with great nakhl in the corner at right, lit up in green

Avenue leading to the Amir Chaghmagh Mosque

I've heard that for reasons to do with its weight and condition this huge nakhl doesn't budge now.

The mourning decorations of Ashura are striking, consisting of a black background with vivid red, green, white and purple lettering.

The courtyard of the Amir Chaghmagh mosque also mourns some more recent heroes, with an inscription that looks like the symbol of the Basij militia, though I may be mistaken.

In the photo where I'm standing beside the small nakhl, you can see some photos on the wall behind me. Here are a couple close up. Are these the occupants of the heroes' graves?

I suspect this had to do with the Iran-Iraq war of the 1980s, which the Iranians call the 'imposed war' since it was Saddam Hussein's idea to start it. They haven't translated the captions for the tourists.

Amir Chaghmagh has tall minarets, but they aren't the tallest in Yazd.

As a town of low-rise adobe architecture in the middle of the desert, Yazd was potentially hard to find. You wouldn't want to be a silk merchant travelling through the desert for many days and nights back in the day, only to miss the place. The city's maze-like streets made it hard for the locals to find their way around as well. The city had grown very organically, and there were no grand avenues of the kind they have in Isfahan.

Perhaps for that reason, Amir Chaghmagh's minarets are quite tall. And they are surpassed by the minarets of Yazd's sublime Jameh or congregational mosque— meaning the main mosque of a locality, where special Friday prayers are said — which has the highest minarets in all of Iran at 52 metres or 171 feet, and the tallest portal as well.

The other great piety of the Yazd region is Zoroastrianism. After the Muslim conquest of Persia, many of the country's remaining Zoroastrians relocated to the Yazd region. Only gradually did Yazd become a majority-Muslim town and to this day it remains the capital of the Zoroastrian world. Having said that, I don't think Zoroastrians are in the majority anywhere now, save possibly in a few outlying towns and villages of the region.

I visited a Zoroastrian temple and school in the downtown area, where I could see the eternal flame behind glass (unbelievers aren't allowed any closer).

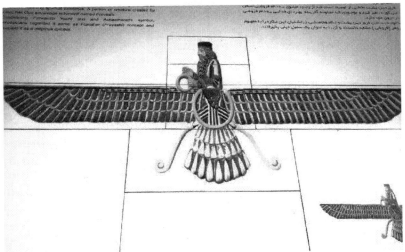

A brightly coloured Faravahar

Zoroastrian Offerings

The Roof of the Temple

Zoroastrian procession with images of Zarathustra and the two Supreme Leaders of the Islamic Republic

Here is the flame, again.

The eternal flame is attended by priests who wear facemasks so that their breath or spit may not accidentally contaminate it. I wonder if modern medical garb, too, was inspired by Zoroastrianism?

And I also went to an important Zoroastrian shrine at a mountain oasis called Pir-e Sabz or the Green Shrine, also known as Chak Chak or 'drip drip' because it constantly drips with water trickling down from the hills.

At the Green Shrine

Outside the city, there are funeral platforms known as dakhma, generally known as the 'towers of silence' in English, where people were laid out to be eaten by vultures. The Zoroastrians of the past thought that this was the most hygienic way to dispose of the dead, as it polluted neither the ground nor the flames, which have a sacred significance in Zoroastrianism as bearers of light.

The funeral work was performed by people called Nesasalar, who lived in a separate village so that if they caught any diseases from the dead people, the whole city wouldn't be infected.

Atop a dakhma, with another dakhma in the background and the city of Yazd behind

A panorama from the same spot, showing nesasalar habitations at left and
more of the city of Yazd behind

We also went hiking in the hills with the intention of getting as
far as we could up Shir Kuh, the highest peak in the region. At
4,055 metres (13,304 feet), Shir Kuh is taller than the highest
mountain in New Zealand, Aoraki / Mt Cook. This wasn't a
serious mountaineering expedition, only a bit of a ramble up the
mist-catching desert mountains. We didn't make it anywhere near
to the top.

But you can see why there are so many mountaineers in Iran, as there are quite serious peaks all over the place, even in the middle of the desert.

There are many other important museums in Yazd, including a museum of Mirrors and Lighting, and a Zoroastrian culture museum.

Yazd is another World Heritage area, like pretty much everywhere I went in Tehran, and very touristy these days. We went to stay in one of Kimi's friends' places. They had moved out of Tehran. Their accommodation and guiding operation was well known. They had a lot of German tourists. There were quite a few guides who took people, and they were very busy.

Which is all very well, but then I found that women couldn't ride bikes. This was surprising, because Yazd is not just touristy, but also a place that has a Copenhagen-like reputation as Iran's capital of cycling. Yet when I wanted to ride a bike, I found that I couldn't. Shocker.

Women are somewhat more secluded in Yazd than in other parts of Iran. They are more likely to wear black chadors than in Tehran (save perhaps in places like Taft, which seem to have a larger proportion of Zoroastrians), and my guide also told me that funeral notices for women aren't displayed publicly. The city has a very low incidence of divorce; officially that's because it is 'family-oriented', but could it be that divorce is regarded as somehow socially unacceptable?

But it wasn't just old ways of the desert, slow to change, that stood in my way. In 2016, Iran's Supreme Leader, Ali Khamenei'i, had also issued a proclamation against women riding bicycles: a proclamation that applied to all of Iran. It followed a debate among clerics as to whether the practice of women riding bicycles was un-Islamic.

The Koran and its surrounding Hadith, a body of early Islamic sayings and commentaries, were silent on the topic. But the clerics decided that the sight of women on bikes was not something Muhammad or the other founders would have approved of, had they been alive to witness the spectacle. Enforcement of the edict varied from place to place. But even in relatively liberal Tehran, groups of women cyclists were dispersed by the police.

It was a reminder that the Islamic Republic, just when you think that it was starting to become more pragmatic, was still capable of coming up with the sorts of policy that you'd have been more likely to associate with Saudi Arabia.

Where, ironically, women *are* now allowed to ride bikes.

And then I found photos of a wealthy Iranian woman who rode a motorbike across Iran. Is it a question of money?

While I was in Yazd, I met a guy who had an app to learn English and had started corresponding with a woman from Melbourne who wanted to learn Persian. They fell in love, and she had been in Iran for a month.

Anyway, he told me he worked in Iraq, and that he had plans which showed that Iran was accepting Russian nuclear waste in return for the use of Russian satellites and military technology.

Iran does have a nuclear waste storage facility near the industrial city of Arak, but officially it is tiny.

Putin defended Assad in Syria. He and his clique are officially over the West in general and no longer care what the United States thinks.

The Russians had once expected to be invited into NATO and were not. I would not be surprised if he helps to defend Iran if there is a future war.

I was going to get maps of where the nuclear waste was dumped. I never received them, but it was an interesting conversation nevertheless.

I also read that American Christian Television was making itself known by beaming information into Iran. Trying to convert Iranians away from Islam is a serious offence in the Islamic Republic, yet obviously they cannot prosecute transmissions beamed in from afar.

CHAPTER 16

Other places to visit in Iran

A S always, there are lots of places I haven't made it to, and wish I had. The Alborz mountains includes the highest mountain in Iran, Mount Damavand, a volcano which is 5,609 metres or 18,403 feet high. It's a highly prominent peak, towering above its surrounding ranges by 4,667 metres or 15,312 feet.

Another place that tourists like to go to is Hormuz Island, a small island in the Straits of Hormuz, which has an old Portuguese fort and amazingly coloured sands.

A Persian Gulf island that's interesting for completely different reasons is Kish, a resort and free trade zone where the laws of the Islamic Republic are relaxed. Iran is trying to develop Kish as a sort of rival to places like Dubai, and it's an interesting social experiment.

Kashan, a city rebuilt after an earthquake in 1778, boasts what is perhaps the finest collection of Qajar-era architecture in Iran.

Mashhad, the second largest-city in Iran, is located in the remote north-east quite close to Afghanistan.

These are just a few additional sites and it's very much worth checking out other people's views of interesting places to visit!

Conclusion

AND so, I say that our attitude to Iran should be one of 'Make Love Not War'. We do not need another war in the Middle East. Most Iranians are not religious extremists. And the people I met were so worried about the future that they did not want to marry or have children.

Like most other humans on this earth they want to enjoy their life. I do believe most people under thirty are worried about the planet's future and this is as true in Iran, as elsewhere.

Acknowledgements

Thanks to all the people who helped me in Iran, and to my editor, Chris Harris.

As always, any errors that may remain are mine.

Made in the USA
Columbia, SC
16 November 2021

49100308R00172